CONTENTS

Foreword 7

Leaves

White cabbage and pointed cabbagge 9

Kale 14

Napa cabbage 19

Savoy cabbage 21

Tuscan cabbage 25

Brussels sprouts 27

Endive 31

Chard 34

Spinach 39

Bok choy 43

Red cabbage 45

Roots and tubers

Potato 48

Jerusalem artichoke 56

Turnip 60

Carrot 64

Rutabaga 69

Parsnip 72

Parsley root 76

Sweet potato 79

Radish and black radish 82

Beet 87

Black salsify 91

Celery root 95

Bulbs, flowers, seeds, and stems

Artichoke 101

Fava beans 104

Broccoli 107

Cauliflower 111

Asparagus 116

Corn 121

Onions: yellow onion, red onion, shallot and white globe onion,

leek, scallion, garlic 124

Fennel 134

Kohlrabi 138

Celery 141

Beans: green bean, yellow wax bean, velour bean, string bean 145

Fruits

Avocado 149

Cucumber 153

Pumpkin 157

Zucchini 160

Eggplant 165

Bell pepper 169

Tomato 171

Dips and cold sauces 176

FOREWORD

What can be done with celeriac? Or with cooked beetroots left over from yesterday's dinner? Is it possible to put something together using cabbage and a pear?

People are increasingly trying to eat more seasonal, ecologically grown vegetables. We have tried to contribute to that trend by providing recipes and tips on how to create easy and delicious dishes all year round. Not only are there instructions for specific dishes, there are also lots of suggestions about how to make the most of vegetables by a variety of different cooking methods and taste combinations. We have kept the tips general and allowed for your own flexibility and creativity so that everyone can experience how easy it is to cook.

The recipes in this book are not an exact science. Often it makes no difference which sort of onion, vinegar or stock you use. Make the most of what you have at home and don't be afraid to substitute ingredients and use your own ideas. We have also made suggestions of what to eat the vegetables with, but even that you can take with a 'pinch of salt' and follow your own preferences or experiment with something new.

All the dishes are not necessarily vegetarian, but they always have vegetables in focus.

There is so much that is good about vegetables. Not only are they very nutritious to eat and relatively cheap to buy, there are so many varieties to choose between, each with their own special character. They can be prepared in so many different ways: quickly cooked or slow cooked to soak up a well flavored stock. Bake in the oven, deep fry, grill or eat raw—grated, thinly sliced or cut into chunks. In combination with other ingredients the variations are endless. Not to mention all the different seasonings, herbs and spices there are to add.

We have organized this book by type of vegetable so that you can easily find a recipe for something you already have or something you have never bought before but are curious to try. Some of the dishes in the book are intended as sides but many of them work very well as a dish in their own right. Or why not put together a number of small vegetable dishes to make one full meal?

Finally, always make sure you buy the best raw ingredients. It makes it easier to cook good food. Buy vegetables that have been grown in healthy soil without chemicals and growth enhancers. The results will be tastier, more nutritious and better for the environment.

WHITE CABBAGE & POINTED CABBAGE

Cabbage is amazingly flexible. Crunchy and sharp when served sliced raw in salads, soft and yielding when braised over a low heat, and flavorful in stir-fries.

In common with other cabbage varieties, white cabbage is divided into growing seasons: summer, fall, and winter. Summer cabbage varieties grow the fastest. The heads are loose and light as there is plenty of air between their leaves. They are mild in flavor and the leaves are crisp and juicy, almost like lettuce. In contrast, the leaves of fall and winter cabbages are quite hard and leathery, and when the cabbage is ripe, they bind together so tightly there is hardly any air between them. These cabbage heads can be stored over the winter—the closer they are packed together, the longer they will last.

You can tenderize uncooked winter cabbage by rubbing cabbage slices with some salt before combining them with other ingredients. Carrots, kohlrabi, beans, other cabbages, nuts, seeds, dried or fresh fruits, and herbs can be combined with white cabbage in a salad. Avoid using oil and vinegar. Late fall—when the cabbage is ripe and the sugar content at its highest—is the perfect time to pickle raw cabbage.

Cut white cabbage into wedges keeping some of the core intact so that the leaves hold together. Simmer in salted water or stock until soft. White cabbage soup with meatballs or a piece of pork sausage is a forgotten classic. Or shred the cabbage, cover with cream, and simmer until soft. Try frying cabbage instead of boiling it. Browned white cabbage has a completely different flavor.

Its shape distinguishes pointed from white cabbage. It is similar to summer cabbage in both taste and texture, and can be used just like white cabbage.

STORING
White cabbage and pointed cabbage are best stored in the fridge, preferably in a kitchen towel. Blanched or cooked white cabbage can be frozen.

SEASON
Organic cabbage can be harvested from summer to late fall. Pointed cabbage is harvested from summer to early fall.

GOES WELL WITH
White cabbage and pointed cabbage go well with, for example, mushrooms, orange, lemon, apples, raisins, capers, nuts, sunflower seeds, goat cheese, and bacon.

< White cabbage with sesame, sea salt, oil, and lemon.

34 ways of preparing white & pointed cabbage

RAW

With vinegar, oil, and dried herbs

Cut white cabbage into thin slices. Place in a bowl. Rub the slices with salt and season with a splash of vinegar, oil, salt, pepper, and dried herbs, such basil, thyme, and oregano.

With sesame, sea salt, oil, and lemon

Dry-roast white and black sesame seeds in a skillet. Grind coarsely and combine with sea salt. Sprinkle the seeds over thinly shredded white cabbage and drizzle with oil. Season with lemon juice and pepper.

With dill, parsley, capers, and vinaigrette

Cut white cabbage into thin slices. Place in a bowl along with chopped dill, parsley, and capers. Whisk together 1 part lemon juice or vinegar, 2–3 parts olive oil, salt, and pepper. Add the vinaigrette to the bowl.

With kohlrabi, yogurt, mint, and honey

In a bowl, combine equal parts of thinly shredded cabbage and kohlrabi. Stir in yogurt and generous amounts of finely chopped mint. Flavor with runny honey, salt, and pepper.

With soy and sweet chili

In a saucepan, bring equal parts light soy and sweet chili sauces to the boil. Pour the sauce over shredded white cabbage and leave to marinate for 10–15 minutes. Goes well with chicken.

With kale, apple, red onion, almonds, and vinaigrette

Cut white cabbage into thin slices. In a bowl, combine with blanched and shredded kale, thinly sliced apple, red onion, and roasted blanched almonds. Whisk together 1 part apple cider vinegar, 3 parts olive oil, salt, and pepper. Add the vinaigrette to the cabbage mixture.

With pear, walnuts, and vinaigrette

Cut white cabbage into thin slices. In a bowl, combine with thinly sliced pears and chopped walnuts. Whisk together 1 part vinegar and 3 parts olive oil, salt, and pepper. Carefully fold the vinaigrette into the bowl.

With carrot, mustard, vinaigrette, and sunflower seeds

In a bowl, combine shredded white cabbage with grated carrots. Whisk together 1 part Dijon mustard, 1 part vinegar, 3 parts olive oil, salt, and pepper. Fold the vinaigrette into the bowl and sprinkle with plenty of roasted sunflower seeds.

With carrot, yogurt, garlic, cumin, and chili powder

In a bowl, combine shredded white cabbage with grated carrots. Stir a splash of olive oil into yogurt, grate in some garlic, and season with a pinch of cumin and chili powder. Fold into the vegetables.

With rhubarb, vinaigrette, honey, and almonds

In a bowl, combine shredded white cabbage with very thinly shredded rhubarb. Whisk together 1 part white wine vinegar, 3 parts oil, honey, salt, and pepper. Fold the vinaigrette into the bowl. Sprinkle with chopped roasted almonds.

With sauerkraut, onion, mayonnaise, mustard, and parsley

In a bowl, combine shredded white cabbage with sauerkraut and sliced onion. Stir in some mayonnaise. Season with mustard, salt, and pepper. Garnish with chopped parsley.

PICKLE

With vinegar, sugar, bay leaves, mustard seeds, and ginger

Slice white cabbage. Put in a jar with a lid. In a saucepan, boil 1 part vinegar, 2 parts powdered sugar, 3 parts water, some bay leaves, mustard seeds, and finely chopped ginger. Let cool slightly. Cover the cabbage with the liquid, replace the lid, and set aside for a couple of hours. The pickle can be stored in the fridge for up to one month.

BOIL
With butter, parsley, and lemon
Cut white cabbage into thin wedges keeping some of the core intact so the leaves hold together. Cook in a saucepan of salted water until soft. Drain and stir in softened butter, plenty of chopped parsley, and some lemon juice.

With butter, capers, and herbs
Cut white cabbage into rough chunks. In a saucepan bring salted water to the boil with a pat of butter. Add the cabbage and capers, and allow to soften. Season with salt and pepper, sprinkle with plenty of chopped herbs.

With butter, dill, lemon, and black pepper
Cut white cabbage into wedges keeping some of the core intact so the leaves hold together. Cook in a saucepan of salted water until soft. Drain the water and place the cabbage on a platter. Brown the butter in a skillet and drizzle over the cabbage. Sprinkle with chopped dill and grated lemon zest. Season with freshly ground black pepper. Goes well with, for example, white fish.

With molasse, stock, pepper, bay leaves, and thyme
Cut white cabbage into rough chunks. Brown in a skillet with molasses and butter. Transfer the cabbage to a saucepan and cover with meat or vegetable stock. Add peppercorns, bay leaves, and thyme and simmer for 20 minutes, or until the cabbage is soft. Dilute with more stock to make a smooth soup. Season with salt and pepper. Serve the soup with meatballs or boiled sausage, or on its own with wholemeal bread.

With crème fraîche
Chop white cabbage. Cook in a saucepan of salted water until soft. Drain the water, add some crème fraîche, salt, and pepper, and return to the heat to warm through.

With onion, cream, and cranberry
Fry sliced white cabbage in a skillet with butter and sliced onion until soft. Add a generous splash of cream and simmer. Season with salt and pepper, then stir in some raw cranberries. Goes well with, for example, beef or pork steaks.

With butter, white pepper, and cream
Melt and brown butter in a skillet. Add freshly ground white pepper and shredded white cabbage, stir to combine. Cover with cream before the cabbage begins to brown. Reduce the heat and simmer until the texture is creamy and the cabbage tender but still firm. Season with salt and pepper. Goes well with, for example, beef steaks.

FRY
With ginger, garlic, soy, and sweet chili
In a skillet, fry sliced white cabbage over a high heat with finely chopped ginger and garlic in oil. Season with equal parts light soy sauce and sweet chili sauce.

With garlic, lemon, whipping cream or crème fraîche, and dill
In a skillet, fry sliced white cabbage over a high heat with finely chopped garlic and grated lemon zest in butter. Season with salt and pepper, then fold in a dash of whipping cream or crème fraîche. Sprinkle with chopped dill.

With bacon and parsley
Fry some bacon in olive oil until crispy. Add shredded white cabbage and fry for a few more minutes. Season with salt and pepper, and garnish with finely chopped parsley.

With stock and parsley
Cut white cabbage into thin wedges keeping the core intact so they hold together. Boil in a saucepan of vegetable stock until soft. Remove the wedges and drain well. Fry in butter until golden brown on both sides. Season with salt and pepper, then sprinkle with plenty of chopped parsley.

With parsley and hazelnuts
Cut white cabbage into rough chunks. Fry in butter over a high heat. Season with salt and pepper, and sprinkle with finely chopped parsley and coarsely chopped, blanched hazelnuts.

ROAST
With dried red pepper flakes
Cut white cabbage into thin slices and place into a bowl. Add salt, pepper, red pepper flakes and olive oil. Knead in with your hands. Spread the cabbage on a baking tray and grill in the oven until golden.

With root vegetables
Cut white cabbage into rough chunks. Roast together with a selection of root vegetables at 400 °F (200 °C).

With yellow onion, apple, and thyme
Cut white cabbage and yellow onions into rough chunks. Place into an ovenproof dish with chopped apples, oil, salt, and pepper. Roast at 400 °F (200 °C) for 15–20 minutes, or until soft and golden brown. Sprinkle with chopped thyme toward the end of the cooking time.

With olive oil and white wine
Chop white cabbage and place in an ovenproof dish. Add olive oil and a splash of white wine. Season with salt and pepper. Roast the cabbage at 400 °F (200 °C) until soft and golden brown. Serve with mayonnaise and chopped parsley.

With goat cheese
Cut white cabbage into wedges, keeping some of the core intact so it holds together. Place the wedges in an ovenproof dish with oil, salt, and pepper. Crumble over plenty of goat cheese. Roast at 400 °F (200 °C) for 10–15 minutes, or until soft and golden.

With thyme and butter
Cut white cabbage into wedges, keeping some of the core intact so it holds together. Place on a baking tray, season with salt and pepper, and sprinkle with thyme. Dot the cabbage with butter. Roast at 400 °F (200 °C) for 30 minutes, or until soft and golden brown.

With stock, bacon, and leek
Cut white cabbage into wedges, keeping some of the core intact so that it holds together. Moisten an ovenproof dish with chicken stock. Add the wedges, sprinkle with chopped bacon, and sliced leeks. Roast at 400 °F (200 °C) for 15–20 minutes, or until the cabbage is soft and the bacon crispy.

With thyme and orange
Cut white cabbage into wedges, keeping some of the core intact so it holds together. Brown the wedges in butter in a skillet. Add orange juice and bring to the boil. Season with salt and pepper, and sprinkle with fresh thyme. Roast at 400 °F (200 °C) for about 20 minutes, or until soft. Add grated orange zest.

With leek, cream, butter, and dill
Cut white cabbage into wedges keeping some of the core intact so they hold together. Place in an ovenproof dish with coarsely sliced leeks. Pour over cream and top with butter, salt, and pepper. Bake in the oven at 400 °F (200 °C) for 15–20 minutes. Sprinkle with chopped dill.

BROIL
Whole with flavored butter and bread croutons
Rub olive oil, salt, and pepper into a head of pointed cabbage. Wrap in aluminum foil and cook under the broiler until soft. Halve the cabbage and serve with croutons and flavored butter (see page 179).

< White cabbage with olive oil and white wine.

KALE

Kale is a type of cabbage available with green or violet leaves (the latter is known as purple kale). Depending on the variety you choose, the leaves are more or less crisp.

Cut or break off the leaves from the coarse stems. The leaves can be eaten raw, but they are chewy and the flavor is not particularly appetizing. Shred the leaves very thinly or mix them into a salad, if you want to eat them raw. Otherwise, cook the kale in salted water to enhance its flavor and soften the leaves. Kale can also be blanched and added to salads or other dishes, such as pasta.

Kale will add a strong flavor and texture to soups and stews. Add the leaves at the end of the cooking time. You can also sauté kale or sprinkle it raw over root vegetables and then roast them in the oven until crispy. Deep-fried or oven-roasted and salted kale chips are tasty, crispy, and a great addition to a platter of appetizers.

Do not forget that kale shrinks a bit during cooking.

STORING
Kale is resistant to cold. Store in the fridge wrapped in a towel, preferably after spraying it with cold water. Or blanch, chill in iced water, and freeze.

SEASON
Kale is a hearty vegetable that can be planted from late spring through early summer and harvested continuously. It produces leaves until the first true frost. Greenhouse varieties are grown year-round.

GOES WELL WITH
Kale goes well with potatoes, root vegetables, onion, garlic, lemon, apple, pear, nuts, vinegar, honey, mustard, cream, goat cheese, egg, and bacon.

Kale with Parmesan, garlic, basil, lemon, and pasta. >

22 ways of preparing kale

RAW

With vinaigrette and sunflower seeds

Finely chop kale leaves. In a bowl, combine the kale with coarsely grated carrot and sliced red onion. Whisk together 1 part Dijon mustard, 1 part red wine vinegar, 3 parts oil, salt, and pepper. Pour the vinaigrette into the bowl and stir. Sprinkle with roasted sunflower seeds.

BOIL

With olive oil, Parmesan, garlic, basil, lemon, and pasta

Finely chop kale leaves. Boil for a few minutes in a saucepan of salted water. Drain thoroughly. In a blender, process the kale to a smooth purée with olive oil. Stir in grated Parmesan cheese, crushed garlic, shredded basil, and lemon juice. Stir into freshly cooked pasta.

With peanuts, garlic, oil, Parmesan, and lemon

Finely chop kale leaves. Boil for a few minutes in salted water, then drain. Put into a bowl and combine with unsalted peanuts, crushed garlic, and oil. Stir in grated Parmesan cheese and season with grated lemon zest, salt, and pepper. Goes well with roasted vegetables.

With stock and cream or crème fraîche

Cut kale into slices and blanch the leaves, then sauté them in butter in a skillet. Add cream or crème fraîche, and simmer for a few minutes. Season with salt and pepper. Goes well with ham, meatballs, and bacon.

With pasta

Fold shredded kale leaves into pasta just before the end of the cooking time.

With onion, ground venison, thyme, and cream

Sauté finely chopped onion in butter until soft. Stir in ground venison and fresh thyme, and cook for a few minutes. Add a dash of cream and bring to the boil. Season with salt and pepper. Add thinly sliced kale and cook for a few more minutes.

With carrot, butter, and orange

Chop carrots into equal-sized pieces. Boil in a saucepan of salted water until soft. Drain and add a pat of butter to the pan. Add shredded kale leaves and grated orange zest. Season with salt and pepper.

In soups and stews

Shredded kale leaves add a rich flavor to soups and stews. Stir the leaves into the saucepan at the end of the cooking time.

With cabbage and stock

Chop kale and cabbage leaves. Boil in a saucepan of vegetable stock until soft.

With cabbage, apple, and vinaigrette

Cut kale into slices. Boil for a few minutes in a saucepan of salted water. Drain thoroughly. In a bowl, combine the kale with shredded cabbage and coarsely grated apples. Whisk together 1 part apple cider vinegar, 3 parts olive oil, salt, and pepper. Add the vinaigrette to the bowl.

With onion, apple, and cream

Melt butter in a saucepan, then add shredded kale leaves, sliced onion, and diced apple. Add some cream and cook until soft. Season with salt and pepper. Goes well with, for example, with pan-fried steaks.

FRY
With garlic
Cut kale into thin slices. In a skillet, sauté crushed garlic in olive oil for a few minutes. Add the kale and cook for a few more minutes. Season with salt and pepper.

With garlic and almonds
Roughly chop kale. Sauté in a skillet with olive oil and crushed garlic until crisp. Sprinkle with plenty of dry-roasted almonds. Season with salt and pepper.

With carrot, onion, and sunflower seeds
Thinly slice kale. Sauté sliced or diced carrots in a skillet with butter until the carrots have softened or turned golden brown. Add kale and sliced onion, and sauté for a few more minutes until soft. Season with salt and pepper, and sprinkle with sunflower seeds.

With cauliflower and garlic
Cut cauliflower into small florets. Sauté in a skillet with oil until soft. Add chopped kale leaves and crushed garlic, and sauté for a few more minutes. Season with salt and pepper.

With pork belly or bacon
Coarsely chop kale. Fry the pork belly or bacon, then add the kale, and fry until it is soft. Season with salt and pepper.

With leek, egg, and cheese
Slice kale into strips. In a skillet with olive oil, sauté the kale and sliced leeks. In a bowl, whisk together eggs, a dash of water, salt, and pepper. Pour the mixture over the kale. Using a turner, pull the eggs from the edges toward the center. Repeat several times. Lower the heat and cook until the eggs have almost set. Sprinkle the omelet with grated cheese and fold in half before serving.

With mushrooms, yellow onion, and garlic
Slice kale into strips. In a skillet with oil and butter, sauté the mushrooms with chopped, yellow onion and garlic. Add the kale and sauté for a few more minutes, or until soft. Season with salt and pepper.

ROAST
As chips
Tear kale into pieces. Place in a bowl and toss with olive oil and sea salt. Spread kale on a baking tray covered with parchment paper and bake at 300 °F (150 °C) for about 20 minutes, or until crispy.

With root vegetables
Roast root vegetables at 400 °F (200 °C) for about 20 minutes, or until soft and golden brown. Chop kale. Toss in olive oil and sprinkle over the root vegetables toward the end of the roasting time for very crispy kale chips.

In lasagna
Add a layer of finely chopped kale to a vegetable lasagna.

DEEP-FRY
As chips
Deep-fry the kale leaves in hot oil. Take care, as the oil might splash. Drain on paper towels. Season with salt.

See also the black salsify tips on page 92.

NAPA CABBAGE

Napa cabbage, also known as Chinese cabbage, had its heyday during the 1970s and 1980s, when it mostly appeared shredded in salads. Thankfully, Asian cooking has shown that this very crispy and juicy cabbage has many more delicious uses.

Napa cabbage is mild and best combined with other flavors, preferably spicy notes. The frilly leaves, which soak up both taste and liquid, are a great addition to a delicious wok dish or in chili-flavored kimchi, for example. Shredded napa cabbage is also a good soup and stew ingredient. Add it at the last minute of the cooking time.

Napa cabbage can also be shredded into a salad. To make it extra tasty, soak the cabbage slices in vinaigrette for a while before combining them with the other salad ingredients. If you chill the strips in iced water for a short time, they become even crispier.

STORING
Store napa cabbage in the fridge, preferably in a damp cloth. Napa cabbage is not suitable for freezing.

SEASON
Napa cabbage is harvested from early to late fall. It can be stored until late winter/early spring.

GOES WELL WITH
Napa cabbage goes well with, for example, chili, ginger, garlic, soy, lemon, and bacon.

< Napa cabbage with soy sauce.

11 ways of preparing napa cabbage

RAW
In a green salad
Make a green salad crispier by mixing in a little shredded napa cabbage.

With red onion, apple, and lemon dressing
Cut napa cabbage into strips, and combine with sliced red onion and coarsely grated apple. Whisk together 1 part squeezed lemon, 2 parts olive oil, salt, and pepper. Pour the lemon dressing into the bowl and stir.

With soy and sweet chili
In a small saucepan, simmer together equal parts light soy and sweet chili sauces. Pour the mixture over shredded napa cabbage and let stand for 10–15 minutes.

With carrot, leek, rice vinegar, ginger, and sesame seeds
Cut napa cabbage into slices. In a bowl, combine it with grated carrot and sliced leek. Whisk together 1 part rice vinegar, 2 parts olive oil, a dash of sesame oil, grated ginger, salt, and pepper. Fold the vinaigrette into the salad and sprinkle with sesame seeds.

With rice vinegar, soy, ginger, chili, and cilantro
Cut napa cabbage into thin slices. Put them in a bowl. Whisk together rice vinegar, a dash of oil, light soy sauce, grated ginger, minced chili, cilantro, and a little salt. Pour the marinade into the bowl and stir to combine. Allow to marinate for about one hour. Goes well with rice or noodles.

BOIL
In stock, soups, and stews
Add shredded napa cabbage to stocks, soups, and stews.

With bacon, butter, and lemon
Cut napa cabbage into wedges. Boil rapidly in a saucepan of salted water or vegetable stock. Serve with crispy bacon, melted butter, and a little lemon juice.

FRY
With garlic
Heat oil in a wok. Add coarsely shredded napa cabbage and sliced garlic. Stir-fry quickly until the cabbage is hot and crispy. Season with salt and pepper.

With string beans, leek, sesame, ginger, and chili
Heat oil in a wok. Add shredded napa cabbage, string beans, and leek. Stir-fry quickly until the cabbage is hot and crispy. Season with sesame oil, chopped ginger, chili, sesame seeds, salt, and pepper.

With soy sauce
Cut napa cabbage into wedges. Fry quickly in a skillet with oil. Sprinkle with light soy sauce, salt, and pepper.

With oyster mushrooms and garlic
Chop oyster mushrooms and fry in oil and butter until golden brown. Season with salt and pepper. Grate in plenty of garlic and add coarsely chopped napa cabbage.

See also the bok choy tips on page 44.

SAVOY CABBAGE

Savoy cabbage is a super-versatile favorite, and the perfect accompaniment to traditional family dishes as well as spicy Asian recipes. Its mild taste is the ideal partner to stronger, spicy flavors, and its ridged leaves absorb both flavor and liquid, so they work well in a flavorsome wok dish or a chili-based recipe. To prepare savoy cabbage, pull any tough outer leaves off the cabbage head and discard. Cut the cabbage in half, then remove the hard inner core. Rinse the leaves and shred as finely as you can.

Shredded savoy cabbage works well in soups and stews—add toward the end of the cooking time to retain its texture. Savoy cabbage can also be washed, shredded, and served raw in healthy salads—it is packed with nutritional goodness. Plunging the shredded leaves into iced water will make them extra crispy. Marinating the leaves in vinaigrette adds more flavor.

STORING
Savoy cabbage should be protected from drying out. Blanched or cooked savoy cabbage is fine to freeze.

SEASON
Savoy cabbage is hardy in cold temperatures. It is planted in early spring or early fall for harvesting while the weather is cool but not freezing.

GOES WELL WITH
Savoy cabbage goes well with, for example, onion, garlic, parsley, apples, mustard, cream, butter, and goat cheese.

12 ways of preparing savoy cabbage

RAW

With scallion, baby leaf spinach, mustard, and vinaigrette

Cut savoy cabbage into thin slices. In a bowl, combine with thinly sliced scallion and baby leaf spinach. Whisk together 1 part whole grain Dijon mustard, 1 part vinegar, 3 parts olive oil, salt, and pepper. Add to the bowl and stir.

BOIL

With red onion, apple, and vinaigrette

Cut savoy cabbage into slices and boil in a saucepan of salted water. Drain, rinse in cold water, and drain again. Place in a bowl with sliced red onion and chopped apples. Whisk together 1 part apple cider vinegar, 3 parts olive oil, salt, and pepper. Add to the bowl and stir to combine.

In soups and stews

Shredded savoy cabbage adds extra flavor to soups and stews.

With onion, cream, and cranberry

Cut savoy cabbage into slices. Sauté in a skillet with butter and sliced onion until soft. Add a splash of cream and cook for about 5 minutes. Season with salt and pepper, then add fresh cranberries.

With onion, garlic, white wine, stock, and lemon

Cut savoy cabbage into slices. Sauté in a skillet with butter, sliced onion, and garlic until soft. Add a splash of white wine, cover with vegetable stock, and simmer, covered, for about 5 minutes. Season with grated lemon zest, salt, and pepper.

With onion, cream, apple, and hazelnuts

Cut savoy cabbage into thin slices. Sauté in a skillet with butter and sliced onion until soft. Add heavy cream and simmer for a few minutes. Add apple slices, cook until warmed through. Season with salt and pepper, then sprinkle with chopped hazelnuts.

FRY

With leek, garlic, mushrooms, pork, and parsley

Cut the savoy cabbage into slices. Fry in butter together with sliced leek and garlic over a low heat until soft. Place on a platter. Fry mushrooms and diced pork in the same skillet until golden brown. Add to the cabbage. Season with salt and pepper and top with parsley.

With onion, cream, apple, and mustard

Cut savoy cabbage into thin slices. Sauté in a skillet with olive oil, butter, and finely chopped onions until soft. Add cream and simmer until smooth. Add diced apple and season with Dijon mustard, salt, and pepper.

With onion, garlic, crème fraîche, and Parmesan

Cut savoy cabbage into thin strips. Sauté in a frying pan with olive oil, chopped onion, and garlic until soft. Add crème fraîche and fold into freshly cooked pasta. Season with salt and pepper, top with grated Parmesan cheese.

In the wok

Savoy cabbage can be stir-fried in a wok.

ROAST

In cabbage meat loaf or cabbage rolls

Replace white cabbage with savoy cabbage to make meat loaves with cabbage or stuffed cabbage rolls.

With white wine, stock, butter, and thyme

Cut savoy cabbage into wedges. Place on a baking tray or in an ovenproof dish, season with salt and pepper, then add equal parts of white wine and stock. Dot with butter and thyme and bake at 350 °F (175 °C) for 20–30 minutes.

Savoy cabbage with leek, garlic, mushrooms, pork, and parsley. >

TUSCAN CABBAGE

Tuscan cabbage, often referred to as *cavolo nero*, is a member of the kale family. It is available year-round but you may have trouble finding it at farmers' markets or grocery stores as it has many other names, including Tuscan kale, black cabbage, and black kale. Its leaves are a very dark green, almost black, hence its name.

Look for crisp, unblemished leaves, with no holes. Avoid cores that are split or dry. To prepare Tuscan cabbage, remove old or damaged leaves, cut the leaves free from the core and remove any tough stalks. Many leaves will split when you cut them clean from the hard stalk that runs down the center of each leaf. Rinse, then chop and slice.

Tuscan cabbage is milder and has a finer texture than, for example, kale. It can be eaten raw and served very thinly sliced in a salad. However, it is far tastier and softer if boiled quickly over a high heat in a frying pan or wok. Stir freshly boiled Tuscan cabbage into butter, season with salt and pepper, and serve with fish; or cook in a skillet together with onion, garlic, and chili. It also works well in pasta with grated Pecorino cheese, or served simply on a slice of toasted sourdough bread. Shredded Tuscan cabbage can also be combined with other soup ingredients, or sprinkled over oven-roasted root vegetables for the last few minutes of the cooking time until crispy.

STORING
Tuscan cabbage is best stored in the fridge, preferably in a dampened towel to keep it firm. Or blanch, chill in iced water, and then freeze.

SEASON
Harvesting of Tuscan cabbage can start at any stage of development but for best flavor pick after the first frost.

GOES WELL WITH
Tuscan cabbage goes well with, for example, Jerusalem artichoke, potatoes, cauliflower, onion, garlic, lemon, chili, Pecorino cheese, and goat cheese.

< Tuscan cabbage with celery root, garlic, and hazelnuts.

11 ways of preparing Tuscan cabbage

BOIL

With apple, vinaigrette, and walnuts

Cut Tuscan cabbage into slices. Blanch in a saucepan of salted water. Drain, refresh in cold water, then squeeze out the liquid. In a bowl, combine with diced apple. Whisk together 1 part apple cider vinegar, 3 parts oil, salt, and pepper. Add the vinaigrette to the bowl. Sprinkle with roasted and chopped walnuts.

With garlic, cream, and Parmesan

Cut Tuscan cabbage into slices. Blanch in a saucepan of salted water. Drain, let cool, and squeeze out the liquid. Sauté chopped garlic in olive oil; remove before it browns. Add whipping cream and bring to the boil. Stir in the cabbage and grated Parmesan cheese. Season with salt and pepper. Goes well with freshly cooked spaghetti or macaroni.

FRY

With garlic

Sauté crushed garlic in olive oil in a skillet without browning. Add shredded Tuscan cabbage and stir into the garlic oil. Sauté until the cabbage is soft. Season with salt and pepper.

With pear, shallot, and almonds

Cut pears into wedges, and remove cores. Sauté the wedges in a skillet with butter until golden brown. Add shredded Tuscan cabbage and sliced shallots. Fry until soft. Season with salt and pepper, and sprinkle with blanched and chopped almonds.

With bacon and scallion

Fry finely diced smoked bacon in a skillet until golden brown. Add sliced scallions and shredded Tuscan cabbage. Sauté gently. Season with salt and pepper.

With sweet potato, garlic, and chili

Fry finely diced sweet potato in oil and grated garlic until soft and golden brown. Add minced chili and shredded Tuscan cabbage and fry until soft. Season with salt and pepper.

With celery root, garlic, and hazelnuts

Fry finely diced celery root until soft and golden brown in oil and butter. Add sliced garlic and Tuscan cabbage leaves, and fry until crispy. Season with salt and pepper, and sprinkle with chopped hazelnuts.

With mushrooms, garlic, and egg

Fry mushrooms in butter until golden brown. Add shredded Tuscan cabbage and grated garlic and fry gently. Season with salt and pepper. Crack in eggs and fry until they are set. Goes well with sourdough bread.

With potato gnocchi, garlic, and Parmesan

Fry cooked potato gnocchi in a skillet with olive oil until golden brown. Add shredded Tuscan cabbage and sliced garlic. Fry for a few more minutes. Season with salt and pepper, then sprinkle with grated Parmesan cheese.

ROAST

As chips

Shred Tuscan cabbage. Drizzle with olive oil and spread onto a baking tray. Season with salt. Roast for about 10 minutes at 400 °F (200 °C), or until crispy.

In lasagna

Add a layer of shredded Tuscan cabbage to a lasagna.

See also kale tips on pages 16–17 and savoy cabbage tips on page 22.

BRUSSELS SPROUTS

Brussels sprouts resemble miniature and tightly closed cabbage heads.

They are perfectly edible in their raw form; you can peel and eat the leaves, or thinly slice the sprouts and add to a salad. Before preparing, rub the sprouts with a little olive oil and salt. This will make them softer and give them a stronger flavor, whether the sprouts are boiled, sautéed, steamed, or stir-fried in butter or oil.

When boiling whole Brussels sprouts, the outer leaves will cook much faster than the centers. To cook sprouts more evenly, cut them into wedges, slice or peel them, and blanch the leaves in boiling salted water. You can also crush the Brussels sprouts on a cutting board with a heavy pan or rolling pin. The sprouts will "crack," become flat, and open out.

Do not boil Brussels sprouts for an extended period of time as they will lose their lovely color, character, and distinctive flavor.

STORING

Brussels sprouts are resistant to cold and can easily be stored in the fridge, preferably wrapped in a kitchen towel or a vegetable drawer to keep out humidity. You can also blanch them for a few minutes in lightly salted water, and then chill in iced water before freezing.

SEASON

In regions with a mild winter, Brussels sprouts are planted in late summer or fall and can be harvested through winter.

GOES WELL WITH

Brussels sprouts go well with lemon, orange, mushrooms, parsley, garlic, chili, butter, and bacon.

20 ways of preparing Brussels sprouts

RAW
With vinaigrette
Cut Brussels sprout leaves from the core with a small knife. Discard any yellow leaves, thinly shred the remaining leaves, and place in a bowl. In a separate bowl, whisk together 1 part white wine vinegar, 2 parts olive oil, salt, and pepper. Toss the leaves in the vinaigrette.

With pickled onion
Cut Brussels sprout leaves from the core with a small knife. Place in a bowl with pickled shallots, white onion, or red onion. Season with salt and pepper, and drizzle with olive oil. Goes well with roasted root vegetables.

BOIL
Boil whole
Trim Brussels sprouts with a small knife. Place them on a cutting board and crush them with a heavy pan. The sprouts will crack and flatten. Boil in a saucepan of lightly salted water for 5–10 minutes, or until soft. Drain well. Or boil the sprouts for a couple of minutes in lightly salted water, chill in iced water, then freeze.

With butter or olive oil and parsley
Serve cooked Brussels sprouts with a pat of butter or drizzle of olive oil, and a generous amount of chopped parsley. Season with salt and pepper.

With butter and orange
Melt a pat of butter in a pan. Combine the juice and zest of one orange with boiled Brussels sprouts and add to the pan. Season with salt and pepper.

With butter
Cut Brussels sprouts into thin slices. Boil in a saucepan of salted water with a little butter until soft. Drain and season with salt and pepper.

With butter, cream, and potato
Blend cooked Brussels sprouts with butter and cream to make a purée. Combine with mashed potato. Season with salt and pepper. Goes well with baked fish or pork.

With butter, mustard, and parsley
Halve Brussels sprouts and boil in a saucepan of salted water until soft. Drain. Brown the butter in a frying pan and add the sprouts. Season with whole grain Dijon mustard, salt, and pepper. Add a generous amount of chopped parsley. Goes well with meatballs and potatoes.

With vinaigrette, scallion, and ginger
Separate the leaves of the Brussels sprouts with a small knife. Boil in a saucepan of salted water, drain, and refresh in iced water. Toss the leaves in olive oil and fresh lemon juice, chopped scallions, and freshly grated ginger.

With cream and mustard
Reduce cream to a syrupy consistency and add to cooked Brussels sprouts. Season with salt, pepper, and Dijon mustard. Goes well with beef and venison.

With browned butter, soy sauce, and white onion or shallot
Separate the leaves of Brussels sprouts with a small knife. Boil in a saucepan of salted water and drain. Brown a generous amount of butter in a frying pan and season with light soy sauce. Add the leaves together with finely chopped white onion or shallots.

With butter, egg, mayonnaise, Dijon mustard, and croutons
Separate the leaves of Brussels sprouts with a small knife. Boil in a saucepan of salted water. Drain, add a pat of butter, and return to the heat. Season with salt and pepper. Spoon the leaves over halved soft-boiled eggs. Flavor the mayonnaise with Dijon mustard. Serve the Brussels eggs with the mayo and croutons.

In soup
Stir Brussels sprout leaves into a soup just before serving.

Brussels sprouts with vinaigrette; Brussels sprouts with butter. >

FRY
With yellow onion, pear, thyme, and hazelnuts
In a skillet, brown finely chopped yellow onions, thinly sliced pears, and thyme in butter. Add chopped cooked Brussels sprouts and cook for a couple of minutes. Season with salt and pepper. Sprinkle with blanched and coarsely chopped hazelnuts.

With bacon, onion, garlic, and parsley
Pan-fry diced bacon until crispy. Drain on paper towels. Sauté thinly sliced onion and garlic in the same pan. Add chopped cooked Brussels sprouts, and cook for several more minutes. Season with salt and pepper. Top with the bacon and finely chopped parsley.

With mushrooms and onion
In a skillet, sauté mushrooms in butter until golden brown. Add chopped cooked Brussels sprouts and finely chopped onion, and cook for a couple more minutes. Season with salt and pepper. Goes well with an omelet.

With yellow onion and almonds
Separate the leaves of the Brussels sprouts with a small knife. Shred any still attached to the base. In a pan over a low heat, sauté the whole leaves in butter. Fold in thinly sliced yellow onion. Cook for 5–10 minutes, or until they are soft and slightly browned. Add shredded Brussels sprouts and sauté for a few minutes more. Season with salt, pepper, and sprinkle with roasted almonds.

ROAST
With garlic, lemon, and honey
Halve Brussels sprouts and spread on a baking tray or in an ovenproof dish. Whisk together olive oil, crushed garlic, lemon zest, and a dash of honey. Toss the sprouts in the dressing. Season with salt, pepper, and add a pat of butter. Roast at 400 °F (200 °C) for around 15 minutes, or until soft and golden brown.

With sesame seeds and soy sauce
Halve Brussels sprouts and toss in oil, salt, and pepper. Transfer to a baking tray or ovenproof dish. Roast at 400 °F (200 °C) for 15 minutes, or until soft and golden brown. Drizzle with light soy sauce and sprinkle with roasted sesame seeds.

DEEP-FRY
With aioli
Deep-fry whole or halved Brussels sprouts in hot oil. Be careful—the oil might spatter and burn you. Drain on paper towels, season with salt, and serve with aioli.

ENDIVE

Endives, with their distinctive bitter flavor, can be an acquired taste. To broaden the appeal of Belgian endives, a milder variety has now been introduced.

Belgian endives are primarily grown in greenhouses. The compact, oblong heads feature bright yellow or reddish-white leaves. If exposed to sunlight, the leaves turn green and so bitter that much of the endive will be inedible. To prevent this, they are packed into light-blocking boxes, in dark wrapping paper, and should be kept out of sunlight in both the store and your kitchen.

Crispy endive leaves can be eaten raw in salads and tossed in vinaigrettes, or combined with creamier and somewhat sweeter side dishes. Soak the raw leaves in iced water to make them crispier and milder in flavor. When the leaves are cooked—boiled, fried, or broiled—the bitterness is reduced and the flavor is sweeter and subtler.

Cut endives into slices, halve lengthwise, cut into wedges, or cook whole. You can also spoon cream cheese into the ends of individual leaves for a make-ahead finger food appetizer.

Escarole, curly endive, and **radicchio** are other examples of strongly flavored salad lettuce.

STORING
Store wrapped in a kitchen towel in in the fridge.

SEASON
Endives are planted in early spring, for summer harvest. They are also grown as a fall crop, and cultivated year-round in greenhouses.

GOES WELL WITH
Endive goes well with tomatoes, mushrooms, orange, pears, apple, olives, nuts, blue cheese, butter, and bacon.

13 ways of preparing endive

RAW

In salad
Flavor a salad with finely shredded endives.

With lemon and basil
Cut endives into thin slices. In a bowl, turn them in olive oil and flavor with freshly squeezed lemon juice, shredded basil, salt and pepper.

With apple, vinaigrette, and mustard
Thinly slice endives and apples. Whisk together 1 part vinegar, 3 parts olive oil, mustard, salt, and pepper. Toss the salad with the vinaigrette.

With blue cheese and crème fraîche
In a bowl, combine blue cheese with crème fraîche. Serve on endive leaves.

With olive, sun-dried tomato, and garlic
In a bowl, combine pitted black olives, sliced sun-dried tomatoes, and garlic. Season with salt and pepper. Serve on endive leaves.

With baby leaf spinach, walnuts, chive, vinaigrette, and honey
In a bowl, combine endive leaves, baby leaf spinach, chopped walnuts, and finely chopped chives. Whisk together 1 part vinegar, 2 parts oil, honey, salt, and pepper. Toss the salad in the vinaigrette. Goes well with goat cheese.

With white wine vinegar, sugar, and green beans
Combine 1 part white wine vinegar, 2 parts sugar, and 3 parts water in a pan and bring to the boil. Cool. Place endive leaves into the liquid and steep for a couple of hours. Remove the endive and combine with steamed beans in a bowl. Drizzle with olive oil, and season with salt and pepper. Goes well with seafood.

BOIL

With stock
Cook whole or halved endive heads in a saucepan with 1 part white wine, 4 parts stock, and a pat of butter.

With tomato sauce and olive
Halve the endives and cook in a saucepan with tomato sauce until soft. Add olives. Goes well with fish.

FRY

With bacon, onion, lemon, butter, and parsley
Chop the bacon and fry in a skillet until crispy. Drain on paper towels. Cut endive heads in half and briefly fry in the same pan with finely chopped onion. Remove from the heat and let cool. Half-fill the pan with water and lemon juice and simmer until the endives are soft. Drain and season with salt and pepper, add a pat of butter, the bacon, and chopped parsley.

With mushrooms, pasta, parsley, and Parmesan
Sauté mushrooms in a frying pan with olive oil and butter until golden brown. Cut the endives into slices and add to the pan just before the mushrooms are soft. Season with salt and pepper, then fold into freshly cooked pasta. Sprinkle with chopped parsley and shaved Parmesan cheese.

With vinegar and oregano
Halve endives and sauté in a skillet with olive oil until golden brown. Transfer to a platter. Season with salt and pepper, and drizzle with balsamic vinegar. Sprinkle with fresh oregano and serve.

ROAST

With white wine, orange, and rosemary
Cut endives into wedges and arrange on a baking tray. Coat with olive oil, white wine, and orange juice. Season with salt, pepper, and chopped fresh rosemary. Bake at 400 °F (200 °C) for 20 minutes, or until soft.

< Endive with lemon and basil.

CHARD

Chard is related to beets, but the leaves resemble those of spinach and can be prepared in much the same way, that is, served fresh in salads—use the tender sprouts— or steamed, boiled, stewed, or sautéed.

There are many kinds of chard with leaves and stems in varying colors. The most familiar are varieties with green leaves and white veins and stems, but those with stems of yellow, red, pink, orange, or pink are the most beautiful. Unfortunately, some of those fine colors will dull a little when cooked.

Chard tastes fresh and hearty. The leaves and stems are both edible, but the stem needs a longer cooking time. Unless the chard is small and tender, separate the leaves from the stems. If the stems are coarse, peel with a sharp knife, as you would rhubarb. Finely chop the stems and shred the leaves. Boil or fry until soft—place the stems in a pan for a couple of minutes before adding the leaves.

Unlike spinach, chard leaves are robust and keep their consistency well when cooked. But you should expect the chard to reduce quite a bit in volume when cooked.

STORING
Chard is sensitive to heat and dryness, and will easily droop. It should be stored in the fridge, preferably in a kitchen towel, to prevent dehydration. Or cut the leaves into thick slices, blanch them in boiling salted water, chill in iced water, dry, and place in the freezer.

SEASON
Chard can be harvested from summer until it gets cold in the fall.

GOES WELL WITH
Chard goes well with lemon, garlic, chili, Parmesan cheese, nuts, cream, fish, and chicken.

19 ways of preparing chard

RAW
With potato, leek, vinaigrette, and mustard
In a bowl, combine tender chard leaves with chunks of cold, parboiled potato and sliced leek. Whisk together 1 part whole grain mustard, 1 part vinegar, 3 parts oil, salt, and pepper. Toss the salad in the vinaigrette.

With beet
In a bowl, combine shredded chard leaves with oven-roasted beets.

BOIL
With butter and lemon
Cut the chard leaves from the stems with a sharp knife. If they are coarse, peel the stems with a sharp knife. Cut the stems into small pieces and the leaves into thin slices. Cook the stems in a saucepan of salted water, and add the leaves a few minutes later. Drain. Add a pat of butter and turn the chard to coat evenly. Season with salt, pepper, and lemon juice.

With cream, garlic, and Parmesan
Add blanched chard stems and leaves to hot cream seasoned with garlic, grated Parmesan cheese, salt, and pepper.

With leek, garlic, cream, and mustard
Cut chard stems into small pieces and slice the leaves. Sauté the stems in butter in a skillet with sliced leek and crushed garlic for a few minutes or until they turn light golden brown. Add the chard leaves and cook for a few minutes more. Add a dash of cream and cook until creamy. Season with whole grain mustard, salt, and pepper.

In soup
Shredded chard can be added to most soups. Add at the end of the cooking time.

FRY
With lemon
Unless the chard is small and tender, cut the chard leaves from the stems with a sharp knife. If they are coarse, peel the stems with a sharp knife. Cut the stems into small pieces and the leaves into thin slices. Sauté the stems in a skillet with butter or oil, and then add the leaves a few minutes later. Season with salt, pepper, and a dash of freshly squeezed lemon juice.

With garlic, ginger, chili, and soy sauce
Cut chard stems into small pieces and leaves into slices. Heat oil in a skillet. Add chopped garlic, ginger, and chili flakes. Cook for a few minutes. Add the stems and sauté for a few minutes more, then add the leaves and cook until soft. Season with light soy sauce.

With onion, garlic, pasta, and Parmesan
Cut the chard leaves into thin slices and chop the stems. In a frying pan, fry the stems and sliced onion in olive oil until soft, but not browned. Add finely chopped garlic and the chard leaves. Season with salt and pepper. Serve with freshly cooked pasta. Top with grated Parmesan cheese.

With onion, egg, tomato, vinegar, and hot sauce
Cut chard leaves into thin slices. In a frying pan, sauté with finely chopped onion and olive oil. Add a pat of butter, salt, and pepper. Make two small hollows in the chard and crack an egg into each one. Cook for a few minutes more. Add sliced tomato, vinegar, and hot sauce. Goes well with sourdough bread.

With celery root and onion
Cut chard leaves into strips. In a skillet, sauté cooked, diced celery root and finely crushed garlic in butter for a few minutes. Season with salt and pepper.

With cauliflower and golden raisins
In a frying pan, sauté small cauliflower florets in oil and butter until golden. Add chopped chard leaves and raisins. Fry over a high heat, stirring all the time. Season with salt and pepper. Goes well with couscous or other grain-based dishes.

With almonds and feta

Unless the chard is small and tender, cut the chard leaves from the stems with a sharp knife. Cut the stems into small pieces and the leaves into strips. Sauté in a skillet in butter or oil until soft, adding the stems first and then the leaves. Season with salt and pepper. Sprinkle with chopped roasted almonds and crumble some feta cheese over the top. Goes well with cold cuts and toasted bread.

With shallot and anchovies

Slice chard stems and shallots. Coarsely shred the chard leaves. Melt a generous pat of butter in a skillet and add a couple anchovies. Add the chard stems and sliced shallot and sauté for a few minutes without browning. Add the leaves and cook for a few minutes more. Season with coarsely ground black pepper and salt. Goes well with broiled fish and chicken.

With pasta, garlic, tomato, and cheese

Fry cold cooked pasta in oil and butter until it takes on color. Add shredded chard leaves and crushed garlic and sauté for a further minute. Season with salt and pepper. Stir in halved cherry tomatoes and grate over plenty of hard cheese.

With bell pepper, onion, garlic, and olive

Fry chopped bell peppers, sliced onion, and garlic in olive oil. Stir in shredded chard leaves and fry for a further minute. Season with salt and pepper, then stir in some olives. Goes well with tortillas and spicy sausages.

BAKE
In puff pastry with leek, garlic, and feta

Thinly shred the chard. Sauté in a skillet with olive oil, sliced leek, and garlic for a couple of minutes. Season with salt and pepper. Cut the pastry into squares and divide the chard mixture between them. Top with crumbled feta or blue cheese and make into parcels. Bake the parcels in the oven at 400 °F (200 °C) for about 5–10 minutes, or until golden brown.

With potato, garlic, tomato, cheese, egg, and milk

In a skillet, sauté shredded chard and grated garlic with olive oil for a few minutes. Season with salt and pepper. Place cold, boiled potato slices in a greased ovenproof dish. Spread the chard over the potatoes. Top with tomato slices. Sprinkle with grated cheese. Whisk together a mixture of egg and milk (1 egg per ½ cup/120 ml) milk, then pour over. Season with salt and pepper, and bake in the oven at 350 °F (175 °C) for 20 minutes, or until set.

BROIL
With onion, fish fillet, and lemon

Cut chard into slices and combine with sliced onion in a bowl. Season with salt and pepper. Put the mixture onto a piece of aluminum foil and place a fish fillet on top. Season with salt and pepper and fold to make a parcel. Broil until the fish is done, about 10 minutes. Open the parcel and add lemon juice.

See spinach tips on pages 40–41 and bok choy tips on page 44.

< Chard with almonds and feta.

SPINACH

Spinach has coarse, bright green leaves, which can vary from smooth to very "crinkly." Baby leaf spinach has young and tender leaves. Cut the leaves away from their strong central ribs and rinse carefully as soil may be caught in the leaf folds. The thick leaves are well suited to cooking; just keep in mind that they will shrink in volume. The easiest way to cook spinach is to shake the leaves well after rinsing and soften them in a saucepan or skillet with a pat of butter or some oil, then season them with salt and pepper. Or briefly blanch the leaves in boiling water, plunge into iced water, and squeeze out the liquid. Add blanched leaves to risottos, stews, or vegetable soups.

Fry spinach together with onions, garlic, tomatoes, or mushrooms. Serve as it is or use to make an omelet by adding lightly whisked eggs. Fill puff pastry for a pie with a mixture of fried spinach, leek, garlic, and feta cheese. Shredded spinach can also be stirred into a bowl of oven-roasted root vegetables.

Spinach contains nitrates, which can be converted to nitrites in the body, so it should not be given to infants or children under one year old.

Baby leaf spinach has little flavor or texture when cooked. Add raw to pasta dishes just before serving or to mixed summer salads. Wilted leaves regain their firmness when briefly placed in iced water.

STORING
Rinse spinach, shake off water, and store in the fridge wrapped in a kitchen towel. Or tie the stems together, blanch in boiling salted water, plunge into iced water, drain, and freeze.

SEASON
Spinach is a cool-season annual. It can be planted in late summer for a fall harvest or early fall for a winter harvest.

GOES WELL WITH
Spinach goes well with, for example, mushrooms, beets, garlic, lemon, chili, ginger, nutmeg, goat cheese, feta cheese, eggs, fish, and bacon.

< Spinach with mushrooms and red onion.

24 ways of preparing spinach

RAW

With red onion, vinaigrette, feta, and pine nuts
Combine baby leaf spinach and sliced red onion in a bowl. Whisk together 1 part red wine vinegar, 3 parts olive oil, salt, and pepper. Add the vinaigrette to the spinach. Crumble over feta cheese and sprinkle with roasted pine nuts.

With iceberg lettuce, parsley, olive oil, garlic, and lemon
Purée baby leaf spinach, iceberg lettuce, and parsley with olive oil to make a green sauce. Flavor with grated garlic and lemon juice, and season with salt and pepper.

In soups
Stir chopped spinach into vegetable soups to add an appetizing green color.

With pasta
Add shredded spinach or baby leaf spinach to freshly boiled pasta.

In lasagna
Add a layer of spinach to a lasagna.

With roasted vegetables
Add shredded spinach or baby leaf spinach to roasted root vegetables.

BOIL
Blanch
Dip spinach in a pan of boiling salted water. Drain and plunge into a bowl of iced water. Squeeze out the liquid.

With butter
Melt butter in a saucepan. Add chopped spinach and allow the leaves to soften. Season with salt and pepper.

In risotto with butternut squash
Add puréed butternut squash and blanched spinach to the risotto.

With onion, garlic, white wine, stock, and cream
Fry chopped onions and garlic in oil. Add a splash of white wine and top up with stock. Cook for about 10 minutes. Add cream and chopped spinach, and cook for a few more minutes. Add stock to make a soup. Season with salt and pepper. Delicious with hard-boiled eggs.

With stock
Bring vegetable stock to a boil in a saucepan. Add chopped spinach and stir well. Season with salt and pepper.

With onion, cream, and nutmeg
In a skillet over a low heat, sauté chopped spinach and finely chopped onion until soft. Cover with cream and simmer. Season with grated nutmeg, salt, and pepper.

FRY
With leek, cream, and Parmesan
Shred spinach and fry quickly with butter and sliced leek. Add cream and simmer. Add grated Parmesan cheese. Season with salt and pepper. Goes well with, for example, fish.

With garlic, Pecorino, toast, and egg
Shred spinach and fry for a few minutes in a skillet with olive oil and thinly sliced garlic. Season with salt and pepper, then sprinkle with grated Pecorino cheese. Serve on slices of toast and top with a fried egg.

With bacon, apple, and onion
Cook bacon in a skillet until crispy. Add thinly sliced apple and chopped onions, and fry until soft and golden brown. Fold in shredded spinach. Season with salt and pepper. Goes well with, for example, fried fish.

With tomato, garlic, pasta, and Parmesan
Fry halved cherry tomatoes and sliced garlic in olive oil for a few minutes. Add shredded spinach. Fry for a few more minutes. Season with salt and pepper. Fold into freshly cooked pasta with grated Parmesan cheese.

With onion, egg, cream cheese, and salmon
Shred spinach and fry together with sliced onions and butter. In a bowl, whisk together eggs, a splash of water, salt, and pepper. Pour the mixture over the spinach. With a turner, pull the egg away from the edges of the skillet toward the center a few times. Lower the heat and fry the omelet until the eggs are almost set. Add cream cheese and place smoked salmon on top. Fold in half.

With mushrooms and red onion
Chop mushrooms. Fry in oil and butter until golden brown. Add chopped spinach and allow to soften. Add halved, then thinly sliced red onion. Season with salt and pepper.

With onion, cream cheese, horseradish, and minute steak or salmon
Shred spinach and fry in butter together with finely chopped onion. Transfer to a bowl and let cool. Stir in the cream cheese and grated horseradish. Place a pat of the mixture on top of minute steaks, and quickly fry on both sides.

With leek, peas, and egg
Fry thinly sliced leek in butter without browning. Stir in garden peas and heat through. Add plenty of chopped spinach and cook to soften. Season with salt and pepper, and sprinkle with chopped eggs. Goes well with fish.

With béchamel sauce, bread, ham, mustard, and cheese
Stir shredded spinach into a hot, thick béchamel sauce. Warm through, then let cool. Spread the mixture onto sliced sourdough bread. Add a few slices of smoked ham, some Dijon mustard, and sprinkle with grated hard cheese. Bake in the oven at 400 °F (200 °C) until the cheese turns golden brown.

BAKE
With salmon, cream, and Parmesan
Place a layer of chopped spinach in the base of a greased ovenproof dish. Place salmon on top. Pour over plenty of cream. Season with salt and pepper, and sprinkle with grated Parmesan cheese. Bake in the oven at 400 °F (200 °C) for about 20 minutes, or until the fish is done.

In puff pastry with leek, garlic, and feta cheese
Cut spinach into strips. Fry in olive oil with sliced leeks and garlic. Season with salt and pepper. Cut puff pastry into small squares and spread spinach mixture on top. Crumble over feta cheese and shape into parcels. Bake in the oven at 400 °F (200 °C) for 10–15 minutes, or until golden brown.

With egg, milk or cream, and potato
Whisk eggs and milk together—use 1 egg to ½ cup (120 ml) milk or cream. Add a couple of chopped spinach leaves and mix until smooth. Season with salt and pepper. Place a layer of cold sliced boiled potatoes in the bottom of a greased ovenproof dish. Pour in the egg mixture and bake at 350 °F (175 °C) for about 20 minutes, or until the eggs have set. Goes well with, for example, gravlax or smoked fish.

See also the chard tips on pages 35 and 37 and the bok choy tips on page 44.

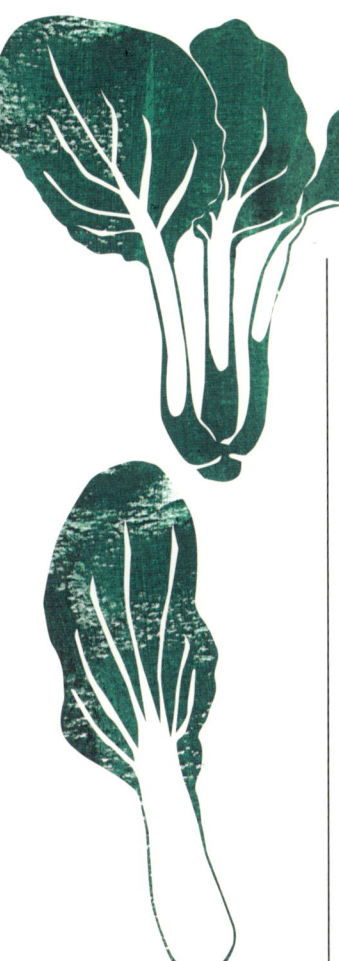

BOK CHOY

Bok choy, or pak choi, has white or light green, thick, juicy stems with a taste and texture similar to napa cabbage. The plain, dark green leaves retain both color and texture during cooking.

Bok choy can be prepared like chard, boiled in stock and soups, or sautéed with garlic and mushrooms. If the bok choy is large, it's a good idea to cut the leaves from the stems and give the stems some extra time in the saucepan or skillet. Often it's the crispness of the stems that gives the vegetable its main appeal.

Bok choy does not have a strong flavor when raw, and it can be shredded and eaten as a salad. The leaves can be marinated in soy sauce or a citrus vinaigrette before being mixed into the salad, to give it more character.

Other spicy flavors, such as chili, ginger, garlic, and vinegar, can give an extra lift to this mild Asian cabbage. If you grow your own bok choy, the plant's flowers can be enjoyed together with other ingredients in a salad or stir-fry.

STORING
Store bok choy in a kitchen towel in the fridge, or cut bok choy leaves into coarse strips, blanch, refresh in iced water, dry, and then freeze.

SEASON
Bok choy harvest time depends on the variety. Mostly it is harvested between late summer and early fall.

GOES WELL WITH
Bok choy goes well with beets, mushrooms, leek, garlic, chili, ginger, lemon, sesame, tofu, vinegar, and soy.

< Bok choy with stock, ginger, yellow onion, garlic, parsnip, carrots, broccoli, and noodles.

12 ways of preparing bok choy

BOIL
In soups and stews
Slice bok choy and add to soups or stews during the final minutes of cooking.

With stock, ginger, yellow onion, garlic, parsnip, carrot, broccoli, and noodles
In a saucepan, boil vegetable stock with finely chopped ginger, sliced yellow onions, and garlic. Peel and slice parsnips and carrots, and add to the pan together with broccoli florets and noodles and cook until soft. Add shredded bok choy and cook until soft. Goes well with broiled chicken or fish.

FRY
With soy, ginger, lemon, and sesame seeds
In a bowl, season light soy sauce with finely chopped ginger and lemon juice. Slice bok choy and sauté in a skillet with oil and sprinkle with roasted sesame seeds. Serve with the sauce. Goes well with rice and tofu or chicken.

With garlic and anchovies
Slice bok choy and fry in olive oil with finely crushed garlic and coarsely chopped anchovies. Season with pepper. Goes well with broiled or fried fish.

With beet, leek, garlic, and vinegar
Cut freshly boiled beets into wedges and place in a bowl. Slice bok choy and sauté quickly in oil with thinly sliced leek and garlic. Add to the bowl. Drizzle with balsamic vinegar, and season with salt and pepper.

With chili, soy, and peanuts
Cut bok choy into large chunks. Fry quickly in oil with ground chili powder. Drizzle with light soy sauce and sprinkle with salted peanuts. Goes well with rice or noodles.

With mushrooms, red onion, and garlic
Sauté the mushrooms in olive oil until golden brown. Add coarsely chopped bok choy, finely chopped red onion, and garlic, and cook for a few minutes more. Season with salt and pepper. Goes well with fried eggs.

With soy and sweet chili
Mix equal parts of soy and sweet chili sauces in a bowl. Cut bok choy into wedges. Sauté quickly in olive oil, add the sauce to the skillet, and heat through.

With orange, soy, olive oil, ginger, and garlic
In a bowl, whisk together equal parts orange juice, light soy sauce, and olive oil. Season with finely chopped ginger and garlic. Cut bok choy into wedges and sauté over a high heat in olive oil, then spoon over the sauce.

With teriyaki sauce, ginger, and lime
Cut bok choy into wedges. Sauté in oil for a couple of minutes, add teriyaki sauce and bring to the boil. Season with finely chopped ginger and grated lime zest. Goes well with rice as a side dish.

With cucumber, red onion, vinegar, and parsley or dill
Cut bok choy stems into strips and the leaves into pieces. Sauté stems in olive oil with ¼-inch (6 mm) thick slices of seeded cucumber and finely chopped red onion for a couple of minutes. Add the bok choy leaves, season with salt and pepper.

In the wok
Coarsely shredded bok choy can be stir-fried with other vegetables. Add just before serving and stir-fry for a few minutes.

See chard tips on pages 35 and 37, and spinach tips on pages 40–41.

RED CABBAGE

In some countries, red cabbage is strongly associated with Christmas meals and tends to be ignored during the rest of the year, although early varieties are available from the summer and late, more compact ones in fall and well into the winter. The leaves are a little coarser and the taste is slightly stronger than white cabbage, but this makes red cabbage more versatile.

Shred the cabbage and spice it up with a fresh vinaigrette, together with apple or orange. Place the shredded cabbage in iced water to crisp up and revive its color, especially if you want to mix it with other salad ingredients. Or use the strong color of the cabbage to turn a creamy cabbage salad purple. All kinds of nuts work well with red cabbage in salads. Raw red cabbage can also be preserved.

If you want to cook red cabbage, retain its crispness by quickly turning slices in a skillet with butter, ginger, and lemon juice, or just fry over a high heat.

Red cabbage keeps its shape during longer cooking times, even when it is boiled in wine or stock until it is really soft. It also provides a fresh and healthy balance to rich dishes, such as roast pork.

Red cabbage can also be oven-roasted. Drizzle small pieces with olive oil before roasting.

STORING
Store red cabbage in the fridge, preferably in a damp towel. Puréed, blanched, and cooked red cabbage can be frozen.

SEASON
Red cabbage, like most cabbage heads, is started indoors and planted out as seedlings after the last frost. The crop is harvested in late summer or early fall. It is available year-round in stores.

GOES WELL WITH
Red cabbage goes well with, for example, apples, lemon, ginger, nuts, raisins, wine, vinegar, bacon, pork, and chicken.

11 ways of preparing red cabagge

RAW
With herbs and vinaigrette
Shred red cabbage and combine with chopped fresh herbs in a bowl. Whisk together 1 part vinegar, 3 parts olive oil, salt, and pepper. Add the vinaigrette.

With pear, vinaigrette, and hazelnuts
Cut red cabbage and pears into thin slices. Mix in a bowl. Whisk together 1 part vinegar, 3 parts olive oil, salt, and pepper. Stir the vinaigrette into the bowl and sprinkle with chopped hazelnuts.

With apple, red onion, parsley, applesauce, and vinaigrette
Shred red cabbage and combine with coarsely chopped apple, thinly sliced red onion, and plenty of shredded parsley. In a bowl, whisk together 1 part applesauce, 1 part apple cider vinegar, 3 parts olive oil, salt, and pepper. Add the vinaigrette and combine.

With cranberry, baby leaf spinach, lemon dressing, and sunflower seeds
Shred red cabbage and combine with dried cranberries and baby leaf spinach in a bowl. Whisk together 1 part lemon juice, 2 parts olive oil, grated lemon zest, salt, and pepper. Stir into the bowl. Sprinkle with roasted sunflower seeds.

With arugula, clementine, vinaigrette, and pumpkin seeds
Shred red cabbage and in a bowl, combine with arugula and clementine slices. Whisk together 1 part red wine vinegar, 3 parts olive oil, salt, and pepper. Add the vinaigrette to the cabbage with roasted pumpkin seeds.

BOIL
With yellow onion, garlic, ginger, and apple juice
Shred red cabbage and sauté in a skillet in butter with finely chopped yellow onion, grated garlic, and ginger. Add a splash of apple juice and simmer until the cabbage is soft.

With bacon, yellow onion, red wine, stock, and herbs
Fry diced bacon in butter until crispy. Add chopped red cabbage and onion, and fry for a few more minutes. Season with salt and pepper. Cover with equal parts red wine and stock, and simmer for 30 minutes. Stir in more butter and chopped herbs.

FRY
With vinaigrette, apple, and parsley
Thinly slice red cabbage and fry in butter until soft and golden brown. Place on a platter. Whisk together 1 part red wine vinegar, 3 parts olive oil, diced apple, salt, and pepper. Pour the vinaigrette over the cabbage and sprinkle with chopped parsley.

With bacon, apple, and chive
Fry bacon until crispy. Add shredded red cabbage and thinly sliced apple, and fry until soft. Season with salt, pepper, and chives.

With ginger, thyme, stock, and orange
Shred red cabbage and fry in butter with grated ginger and thyme until soft. Add stock and cook for a few more minutes. Season with grated orange zest, salt, and pepper.

ROAST
With white wine, lemon dressing, ginger, and chive
Cut red cabbage into wedges. Place in an ovenproof dish and add white wine and olive oil. Season with salt and pepper. Roast in the oven at 300 °F (150 °C) until the cabbage is softened. Increase heat to 400 °F (200 °C) and roast until it is crispy and browned. Whisk together 1 part lemon juice, 2 parts olive oil, grated lemon zest, grated ginger, salt, and pepper. Stir the dressing into the cabbage. Sprinkle with chives.

Red cabbage with apple, red onion, parsley, applesauce, and vinaigrette. >

POTATO

The humble potato is one of our favorite vegetables and around 200 varieties are grown in the United States every year, each with a different flavor and texture. Only a few make their way to our dinner table, but lesser-known varieties—many grown on organic farms—are now being introduced at grocery stores and farmers' markets.

Fast-growing spring potatoes are harvested in early summer when the leaves are still green. It contains more water than a fully grown winter potato and has a delicate, sweet flavor that heralds the summer salad season. The skin is virtually nonexistent, which means that the new potatoes have a short shelf life. Summer-harvested potatoes are a little tougher. The flavor of main crop winter potatoes has developed during their long period in the soil and their tough skins protect them during winter storage.

Potatoes should always be cooked. Boiled potatoes can taste divine, simply served with a pat of butter and a pinch of salt. Or mash the cooked potatoes with a potato masher, add some liquid, and season with herbs, lemon juice, and horseradish or just salt and pepper. Do not mash too hard or long, as it will make the flesh "gluey." The consistency of spring and summer potatoes makes them unsuitable for mashing evenly or puréeing, so smooth potato soups have to wait until the fall.

Use up leftover mash the next day by stirring in eggs and making potato cakes. These go well with cranberries and fried pork. Cut cold, leftover boiled potatoes into smaller chunks and make a creamy potato salad with mayonnaise, or add a vinaigrette dressing. Chopped potatoes can also be sautéed in hot oil and butter until golden brown.

Coarsely grate raw potatoes and form into hash browns. Squeeze out as much of the liquid as possible before shaping and frying them. You can fry raw, thinly sliced potatoes, but larger potato chunks should be boiled before

STORING
The thicker the potato skin, the more durable it is. Store potatoes in a dark and cold environment, but never below 39°F (4°C). If they are stored too close to freezing, the starch will convert to sugar and the potatoes will develop a sweet flavor. If they are exposed to light, they may turn green, and acquire a bitter taste.

SEASON
Fall and winter crops store extremely well in a root cellar. Available throughout the year in stores.

GOES WELL WITH
Potatoes go well with, basically, everything.

frying. Of course, potatoes can also be roasted or baked in the oven, either chopped or whole. Floury potatoes are great for baking; extra-large varieties are now available that have been specially cultivated for oven-baking. To bake a potato, gently prick the skin with a fork before cooking so it doesn't burst.

Creamy potato gratin, deep-fried potato chips, or classic French fries are other ways to prepare the versatile potato. If you only have one bag of potatoes at home, you will never go hungry!

Since potatoes are one of the most heavily sprayed crops in the country, try to find organically grown ones, either at farmers' markets or delivered directly to your home . . . or simply grow your own. You can eat organic potatoes with their skins on, which retains flavor and goodness. Just scrub thoroughly before cooking. Cut green chlorophyll stains out and discard potatoes that are completely green. They are toxic.

POTATO

38 ways of preparing potato

BOIL

With butter and dill
Scrub potatoes and boil in a saucepan with dill stems and salt until soft. Drain, remove the dill, and coarsely mash with a potato masher. Mix in a generous amount of butter and plenty of chopped dill. Season with salt. Goes well with, for example, fried fish.

With red onion, dill, mustard, and vinaigrette
Boil potatoes in a saucepan of salted water until soft. Cut into small chunks and, in a bowl, combine with thin slices of red onion and chopped dill. Whisk together 1 part mustard, 1 part vinegar, 3 parts oil, salt, and pepper. Stir the vinaigrette into the bowl.

With butter, crème fraîche, chive, dill, and lemon
Boil potatoes in a saucepan of salted water until soft. Drain. Coarsely mash with a potato masher. Add a pat of butter, some crème fraîche, and chopped chives and dill. Flavor with grated lemon zest, salt, and pepper.

With beer, stock, butter, thyme, and bay leaves
Put peeled potatoes in a saucepan. Cover with equal parts beer and dark beef stock. Add a large pat of butter, thyme, and bay leaves, cover, and simmer gently for about 20 minutes. Goes well with all kinds of meat, sausages, and mustard.

Mash
In a saucepan of salted water, boil peeled potatoes until soft. Drain. In a second pan, boil milk, or equal parts milk and cream. Add a pat of butter and mash the potatoes with a potato masher, then add enough of the milk to create the desired consistency. Do not work the mash too hard or too long, or it will become sticky. Season with salt and pepper.

< Potatoes with beer, stock, butter, thyme, and bay leaves.

MASH VARIATIONS

✤ Heat cream or milk in a saucepan with fresh thyme and grated garlic. Strain and mash into the boiled potatoes.

✤ Fry finely chopped shallots in butter without browning. Add to the mashed potatoes.

✤ Flavor mashed potatoes with olive oil and grated lemon zest.

✤ Flavor mashed potatoes with grated horseradish.

✤ Flavor mashed potatoes with chopped fresh herbs.

✤ Flavor mashed potatoes with grated hard cheese.

With yellow wax or green beans, parsley, chive, bacon, and vinegar
Slice lukewarm boiled potatoes. In a bowl, combine with the cooked beans, finely chopped parsley, and chives. Cut smoked bacon into cubes and fry until crispy. Pour the pork fat into the bowl and stir together. Flavor with white wine vinegar, salt, and pepper.

With arugula, celery, leek, pesto, and vinegar
Slice cold or lukewarm boiled potatoes. In a bowl, mix with arugula, thinly sliced celery, and leeks. Fold in the pesto and drizzle with white wine vinegar. Season with salt and pepper.

With radishes, gherkin, dill, chive, and lemon dressing
Chop cold or lukewarm boiled potatoes. In a bowl, combine with thinly sliced radishes, diced gherkin, and chopped dill and chives. Whisk together 1 part lemon juice, 2 parts olive oil, salt, and pepper. Stir into the bowl.

With gherkin, yogurt, mayonnaise, garlic, and dill
Chop cold boiled potatoes. in a bowl, combine with cubed gherkins. Add equal parts yogurt and mayonnaise. Season with grated garlic, chopped dill, olive oil, salt, and pepper.

With butter, egg, dill, and chive
Boil peeled potatoes in a saucepan of salted water until soft. Roughly mash. Stir in melted butter, diced hard-boiled egg, chopped dill, and chives. Season with salt and pepper.

With whipped butter
Whisk softened butter in a bowl until white and fluffy. Serve with freshly cooked potatoes.

With butter, bread, dill, chive, and fish or gravlax
Mash freshly cooked potatoes with a pat of butter. Spread the mash onto thinly sliced bread. Dot one half with chopped dill and chives, add a couple of slices of smoked fish or gravlax, then cover with the other half.

With pickled herring, red onion, dill, chive, and butter
Slice hot or cold cooked potatoes and place them on a platter. Chop herring and place on top. Sprinkle with finely chopped red onion, dill, and chives. Spoon over browned butter.

With cream, anchovies, leek, and dill
Heat cream in a saucepan until it thickens. Flavor with chopped anchovy fillets. Add chunks of boiled potatoes, thinly sliced leek, and plenty of chopped dill.

FRY
Mashed potato leftovers
Stir eggs into the cold mash—1 egg to $1/3$ cup (80 ml) mash. Shape the mash into cakes and fry in oil until golden brown. Goes well with cranberries and fried pork.

Boiled potato leftovers
Chop cold boiled potatoes. Fry in plenty of olive oil over a high heat until soft and golden brown. Season with salt and pepper.

With onion, garlic, and herbs
Cut potatoes into thin slices. Fry in plenty of olive oil over a a high heat until soft and golden brown. Reduce the heat, add sliced onion, and garlic, and fry gently. Flavor with salt, pepper, and chopped herbs, such as tarragon and parsley.

With onion, beet, parsley, and horseradish
Cut potatoes into small cubes. Fry in olive oil and butter over a high heat until golden brown. Reduce the heat and fry gently. Season with salt and pepper and place on a platter. Add sliced onion to the skillet and sauté over a low heat. Add cooked beet slices and heat through. Return the potatoes to the pan, sprinkle with parsley and grated horseradish.

With leek, garlic, and baby leaf spinach
Cut potatoes into very thin slices. Fry in butter on a high heat until golden brown. Reduce the heat, add sliced leek and grated garlic, and fry until soft. Add baby leaf spinach, salt, and pepper.

Hash browns
Peel and roughly grate potatoes. Squeeze out as much of the liquid as possible. Place the grated potatoes in a bowl. Season with salt and pepper. Form into several small or one large cake. Fry on both sides in butter until soft and golden brown. Serve with crème fraîche and fish roe.

With parsnip, onion, apple, and parsley
Chop cold cooked potatoes and parsnips into cubes. Fry in butter and oil with chopped onion until golden brown. Add cubed apples and cook for a few more minutes. Season with salt and pepper, sprinkle with chopped parsley.

With herbs
Cut potatoes into thin slices. Fry in oil and a pat of butter until soft. Season with salt and pepper, and sprinkle with herbs.

ROAST
With garlic and thyme
Scrub and thinly slice potatoes. Turn in olive oil, grated garlic, thyme, salt, and pepper on a baking tray. Roast at 440 °F (225 °C) for 15–20 minutes, or until soft and golden brown.

With corn, garlic, chili, and herbs

Cut potatoes into chunks and corn on the cob into 1-inch (2–3 cm) thick slices. Turn both in olive oil, grated garlic, chopped chili, herbs, salt, and pepper on a baking tray. Roast at 400 °F (200 °C) for about 20 minutes. or until soft and golden brown.

With tomato, onion, garlic, salmon, and parsley

Cut potatoes, tomatoes, onion, and garlic into slices. Put on a greased baking tray; season with salt and pepper. Roast at 440 °F (220 °C) for 15 minutes, then reduce the heat to 300 °F (150 °C). Brush salmon steaks with olive oil. Season with salt and pepper. Place the fish on top of the vegetables and return to the oven for about 10 minutes. Sprinkle with parsley.

With garlic, bacon, and savoy cabbage

Place small, unpeeled potatoes on a baking tray and add oil, grated garlic, salt, and pepper. Roast for about 20 minutes at 400 °F (200 °C), or until soft and golden brown. Cube smoked bacon and fry until crispy. Add shredded blanched savoy cabbage. Place the potatoes on a plate and press with a fork to break up. Top with the bacon and cabbage.

With sour cream, cauliflower, and chive

Place small, unpeeled potatoes in oil and plenty of salt on a baking tray. Roast at 400 °F (200 °C) for 20 minutes, or until soft and golden brown. Press the potatoes with a fork to break them up. Pour over some sour cream, cover with grated raw cauliflower and chopped chives. Season with salt and pepper.

With garlic, thyme, and duck fat or butter

Peel potatoes of about the same size and cut in half. Fry the cut surfaces in butter until golden brown. Place in an ovenproof dish with sliced garlic and fresh thyme. Season with salt and pepper. Brush the potatoes with melted duck fat or butter and roast in the oven at 300 °F (150 °C), or until soft. Take out the potatoes, being careful as the fat is very hot. Goes well with, for example, poultry. (Strain the fat once it has cooled down. It can be used again.)

With onion, cream, and milk

Peel potatoes and cut into slices. In an ovenproof dish, combine them with sliced onion, salt, and pepper. Cover with equal parts cream and milk. Roast at 400 °F (200 °C) for about 40 minutes, or until the potatoes are soft and the topping is golden brown.

BROIL
With flavored butter

Rub large potatoes with oil and coarse sea salt. Wrap in aluminum foil and cook under the broiler until soft. Halve and serve with flavored butter (see page 179).

DEEP-FRY
As chips or wedges

Cut unpeeled potatoes into very thin slices or wedges. Rinse in cold water and drain well. When the slices or wedges are completely dry, deep-fry in hot oil until golden brown. Pat dry with paper towels. Season with salt.

Skins

Roughly peel potatoes with a knife so some of the flesh comes off with the skin. Rinse in cold water and drain well. When completely dry, deep-fry the skins in hot oil until golden brown. Drain on paper towels. Season with salt.

Potatoes with sour cream, cauliflower, and chive. >

JERUSALEM ARTICHOKE

Jerusalem artichokes, also called sunchokes, are usually eaten peeled. However, if the skin is light and thin, you may only need to scrub them thoroughly. The skin helps the Jerusalem artichoke stay firm and tasty during cooking. When peeled, place them in water with a squeeze of lemon juice to retain their color and prevent browning.

Flavor and consistency depend on whether Jerusalem artichokes are raw or cooked. Raw Jerusalem artichokes are very mild and nutty. When cooked, the flavor is sweeter and earthier. The sweetness is enhanced if the Jerusalem artichokes were exposed to freezing temperatures before being harvested. If you find the flavor too strong, you might want to balance the Jerusalem artichokes with other starchy vegetables, such as potatoes, or mushrooms.

To eat Jerusalem artichokes raw, cut them into slices—they will add a lovely crispiness to a salad. Dipping the slices into boiling salted water first and chilling them in iced water increases their flavor.

Brown Jerusalem artichoke slices in oil in a pan, before adding stock to make a soup. This accentuates the flavor. To fry Jerusalem artichokes, cut them into small, equal-sized chunks, for even cooking. They can also be roasted on a baking tray with other root vegetables. The skin can be left on if baked whole as it will retain the juices. Pierce Jerusalem artichokes with a fork before baking at a high temperature—once they've taken on a little color, reduce the heat and continue baking until soft.

STORING
Store Jerusalem artichokes in the fridge, preferably in a damp towel. Soaking them in iced water can revive Jerusalem artichokes that have become soft. Chop, then boil them quickly in lightly salted water, chill in iced water, and freeze.

SEASON
Jerusalem artichokes are planted several weeks before the last frost in spring, or in late fall, and harvested after the first hard frost, although it will tolerate several frosts. The crop can be stored in a root cellar.

GOES WELL WITH
Jerusalem artichokes go well with potatoes, kale, spinach, garlic, lemon, apple, thyme, parsley, cream, and bacon.

20 ways of preparing Jerusalem artichoke

RAW
With spinach, vinaigrette, and garlic
Cut Jerusalem artichokes into very thin slices. In a bowl, combine with an equal amount of baby leaf spinach leaves. Whisk together 1 part red wine vinegar, 2 parts olive oil, finely chopped garlic, salt, and pepper. Toss the vegetables in the vinaigrette.

With apple, red onion, and vinaigrette
Cut Jerusalem artichokes into very thin slices. In a bowl, combine with shredded apples and red onion. Whisk together 1 part apple cider vinegar, 2 parts olive oil, salt, and pepper. Toss the salad in the vinaigrette.

BOIL
With crème fraîche, pork belly, and parsley
Peel and chop Jerusalem artichokes, then cook in a saucepan of salted water until soft. Drain and mash the Jerusalem artichokes with crème fraîche. Season with salt and pepper. Add fried cubed pork belly and chopped parsley.

With potato, butter, and parsley
Peel Jerusalem artichokes and potatoes, and cut into small chunks. Boil in a saucepan of salted water until soft. Drain, add a pat of butter, and mash with a potato masher. Season with salt, pepper, and chopped parsley. Goes well with all types of cabbage.

With yellow onion, garlic, thyme, stock, and cream
Cut Jerusalem artichokes into chunks. Brown in a skillet with oil, chopped yellow onion, garlic, and thyme. Cover with stock and cook until completely soft. Add cream until it is the desired consistency. Season with salt and pepper. Top with fried mushrooms. Goes well with pasta or roast vegetables.

FRY
With mushrooms, garlic, and spinach
Cube Jerusalem artichokes and fry in olive oil until soft. Season with salt and pepper. Drain on paper towels. Cut the mushrooms into small chunks. Sauté in butter in the same skillet until golden brown. Add finely chopped garlic, chopped spinach, and the Jerusalem artichokes. Cook for a few more minutes. Season with salt and pepper.

With apple, onion, and parsley
Cube Jerusalem artichokes. Sauté in butter until soft and golden brown. Add thinly sliced apples and coarsely chopped onion, and cook for a few more minutes. Season with salt, pepper, and chopped parsley.

With potato
Peel and coarsely grate Jerusalem artichokes and potatoes. Transfer to a bowl. Season with salt and pepper. Transfer to a tea towel and squeeze out the liquid. Heat butter and oil in a skillet. Shape the Jerusalem artichokes and potatoes into cakes and fry on both sides for about 10 minutes, or until golden brown.

With bacon, romaine lettuce, and vinegar
Cut cold, cooked Jerusalem artichokes into wedges or thick slices. Fry the bacon until crispy. Drain on paper towels. Fry the Jerusalem artichokes in the same pan until golden brown. In a bowl, mix with finely chopped romaine lettuce. Drizzle with sherry vinegar. Season with salt and pepper.

With garlic and kale
Thinly slice Jerusalem artichokes. Fry in oil together with sliced garlic. Add torn kale leaves and fry for a few more minutes. Season with salt and pepper.

In stews
Peel Jerusalem artichokes and cut into even-sized chunks. Sauté in olive oil until soft. Season with salt and pepper. Add to creamy stews.

With mushrooms, garlic, cream, sourdough bread, and parsley

Peel and dice Jerusalem artichokes. Sauté in oil and butter until soft. Add mushrooms and cook until they take on some color. Add chopped garlic and finely chopped onion. Season with salt and pepper. Add a dash of cream and bring to the boil. Spread the mixture onto sourdough bread and garnish with chopped parsley.

ROAST
With garlic and thyme

Slice Jerusalem artichokes or cut into cubes. On a baking tray or ovenproof dish, toss them in olive oil with crushed garlic and thyme. Season with salt and pepper. Roast at 350 °F (175 °C) for about 15–20 minutes, or until they are soft and golden brown.

With butter

Mash cold roasted Jerusalem artichokes to a purée with butter. Season with salt and pepper. Goes well with roasted root vegetables.

With butter, Parmesan, and breadcrumbs

In a bowl, combine equal parts butter at room temperature, grated Parmesan cheese, and breadcrumbs. Spread the mixture onto roasted Jerusalem artichokes and cook at 440 °F (270 °C) until golden brown and crispy.

With browned butter and hazelnuts

In a skillet, brown some butter and fry coarsely chopped hazelnuts. Add roasted Jerusalem artichokes and stir.

With cream cheese, lemon, olive oil, and thyme

In a bowl, stir together the cream cheese, grated lemon zest, lemon juice, a dash of olive oil, and finely chopped thyme. Season with salt, and pepper. Serve with roasted Jerusalem artichokes.

With potato, cream, and milk

Peel and slice Jerusalem artichokes and potatoes, and place on a baking tray or in a greased ovenproof dish. Cover with equal parts cream and milk. Season with salt and pepper. Roast at 400 °F (200 °C) for about 30 minutes, or until soft.

With cream, thyme, and vinegar

Cut Jerusalem artichokes into chunks and place on a baking tray or in a greased ovenproof dish. Roast at 350 °F (175 °C) for about 20 minutes, or until soft and golden brown. Heat the cream and thyme. Blend the Jerusalem artichokes and cream to a purée. Season with salt and pepper, and a dash of red wine vinegar.

DEEP-FRY
As chips

Thinly slice unpeeled Jerusalem artichokes. Deep-fry in hot oil until golden brown. Drain on paper towels. Season with salt.

REFRESH JERUSALEM ARTICHOKES
Jerusalem artichokes don't store well—they easily go wrinkly. You can revive the tubers by placing them in iced water.

INULIN
Jerusalem artichokes contain a starchy substance called inulin, which can cause excess gassiness. The amount of inulin depends on the type of Jerusalem artichokes, the soil they grew in, and when they are harvested. Some experts believe that you can train your stomach to get used to inulin if you eat Jerusalem artichokes often. Inulin will be deactivated if the root is parboiled before cooking. Combining Jerusalem artichokes with fats, such as cream, may also lessen the effect.

TURNIP

Turnips are similar in flavor to radishes, only slightly milder. They also have a slightly bitter aftertaste that, for some recipes, can be counteracted with a pinch of sugar. There are many kinds of turnips, including those harvested in late spring and fall. Early turnips often have a thin edible skin, while the later varieties have a thicker skin that should be removed. The color of the skin varies—completely white, yellow, red and white, with pink and violet top halves, and either white or yellow flesh. Small turnips are the tenderest. If they are larger than 4 inches (10 cm) in diameter, they may have become hard and woody.

Thinly sliced, shredded, and grated raw turnips—even cold, boiled ones—work very well in salads. They can be pickled, fermented, or eaten hot, cooked in salted water, stock, or cream, and added to soups and stews. If you want to fry turnips, either cook them raw or parboiled in a skillet or roast them in the oven. To roast whole turnips, you can leave their skins on—they intensify the flavor. Turnip leaves can also be eaten.

STORING
Store turnips in the fridge in a damp towel. Placing them in iced water can refresh soft turnips. Cut into chunks, cook briefly in lightly salted water, chill in iced water, and freeze.

SEASON
Turnips can be harvested from summer into the fall.

GOES WELL WITH
Turnip goes well with spinach, lemon, apple, garlic, butter, cream, bacon, pork, fish, and chicken.

Turnips with rosemary, sourdough bread, and goat cheese. >

19 ways of preparing turnip

RAW
With lemon, olive oil, and basil
Peel turnips and cut them into very thin slices, then place in a bowl. Salt and let sit for a few minutes. Season with lemon juice, grated lemon zest, olive oil, shredded basil, and pepper.

In salad
Peel and thinly slice turnips, preferably with a mandolin slicer. Place in iced water for a few minutes. Drain and add turnips to a salad.

With baby leaf spinach, vinaigrette, and mustard
Peel turnips and shred or slice them very thin. Combine with baby leaf spinach in a bowl. Whisk together 1 part Dijon mustard, 1 part vinegar, 3 parts oil, salt, and pepper. Toss the salad in the vinaigrette.

BOIL
With vinegar, sugar, bay leaves, and parsley
Peel turnips, cut into very thin slices, and place in a jar. In a saucepan, bring to the boil 1 part vinegar, 2 parts powdered sugar, and 3 parts water with bay leaves. Cool. Pour the liquid over the turnips and marinate for at least six hours. Add chopped parsley.

With butter and dill or chive
Peel turnips and cut into chunks. Cook in salted water until soft. Drain and add a pat of butter, chopped dill or chives, salt, and pepper.

With vinaigrette, honey, and almonds
Peel turnips and cook in a saucepan of salted water until soft. Refresh in cold water and drain. Thinly slice turnips and put on a plate. In a bowl, whisk together 1 part red wine vinegar, 2 parts olive oil, and honey. Season with salt and pepper. Drizzle the vinaigrette over the turnips and sprinkle with roasted flaked almonds.

With cream, garlic, and spinach or chard
Peel turnips and cut into small cubes. Cook in a saucepan with cream and thinly sliced garlic until soft. Pour over shredded spinach or chard. Season with salt and pepper.

With tomato, leek, lemon, and dill
Peel turnips and cut into wedges. Cook in a saucepan of salted water until soft. Drain. Combine with butter, sliced tomatoes, and chopped leeks. Season with lemon juice, salt, and pepper. Sprinkle with chopped dill.

With leek, lettuce, vinaigrette, mustard, pork belly, and croutons
Peel turnips and cut into cubes. Cook in a saucepan of salted water until soft. Refresh in cold water and drain. In a bowl, combine turnips with thinly sliced leeks and shredded lettuce leaves. Whisk together 1 part red wine vinegar, 2 parts olive oil, and Dijon mustard. Toss the salad in the vinaigrette. Season with salt and pepper, and sprinkle with crispy, fried smoked pork belly and croutons.

With onion, stock, apple, and chive
Peel turnips and onion and cut into wedges. Cook in stock until soft. Combine with shredded apples, and chives. Season with salt and pepper

With butter, capers, dill, lemon, and beans
Brown butter in a skillet. Add capers, chopped dill, grated lemon zest, and lemon juice. Turn the turnip wedges and fresh green beans in the butter mixture until coated.

With onion, garlic, milk, lemon, and chive
Peel and chop turnips. Sauté in oil with chopped onion and garlic. Cover with milk, add a pinch of sugar, and simmer for 15–20 minutes, or until the turnips are soft. Drain, refresh in cold water, and purée. Add hot milk until the soup has the desired consistency. Season with salt and pepper. Serve the soup cold with grated lemon zest, chopped chives, and a drizzle of olive oil.

FRY

With bacon and onion

Scrub and chop turnips. Cook in salted water for a few minutes. Drain. Sauté in butter over a low heat with bacon and chopped onion until soft. Goes well with tomato salad and chicken.

With honey, soy, black pepper, and spinach

Peel turnips and cut into wedges. Sauté in olive oil until soft and golden brown. Toss in honey and a few drops of light soy sauce. Season generously with black pepper and stir in shredded spinach.

With pear, thyme, and vinegar

Peel turnips and cut into wedges or halves. Cook in a saucepan of salted water until soft. Drain. Cut pears into thin, wedges; remove the core. Fry in butter with thyme until the pears have turned golden brown and soft. Add the turnip and cook for a few more minutes. Season with salt and pepper and a little vinegar.

With rosemary, sourdough bread, and goat cheese

Peel turnips and cut into thin wedges. Sauté with chopped rosemary in olive oil until soft and golden brown. When cooked, add cubes of sourdough bread. Sprinkle with goat cheese and season with salt and pepper.

With sugar

Peel and slice turnips. Cook in a saucepan of salted water until soft. Drain in a strainer. Coat with sugar and sauté in butter until golden brown. Be careful—they burn easily. Season with salt and pepper. Goes well with chicken.

ROAST

With beet, garlic, and baby leaf spinach

Thoroughly scrub turnips and beets. Cut into wedges and put into separate bowls. Toss in olive oil and grated garlic. Season with salt and pepper. Place next to each other on a baking tray, leaving a small gap between the wedges, and roast at 400°F (190°C) for 20–30 minutes, or until soft. Combine with baby leaf spinach.

With thyme, butter, and herbs

Scrub turnips and cut into halves. Turn in oil and chopped thyme, and transfer to a baking tray. Season with salt and pepper. Bake at 350°F (175°C) for about 20–30 minutes, or until soft. Mix softened butter with chopped herbs and serve with the turnips.

CARROT

A carrot is so much more than the everyday orange vegetable we are familiar with. It can also be yellow, black, purple, red, or white, round, short, long, thick, and wide or thin at the top, and tapered or rounded at the end. It can have loose or dense, white or translucent flesh; it can be sweet, bitter, juicy, or crisp. It can also be a summer carrot that has been harvested early to be eaten raw, or a winter variety, which adds depth of flavor to hearty, warming soups and stews.

There are many ways to prepare and cook carrots. Raw, sliced, grated, juiced, pickled, boiled, sautéed, broiled, deep-fried, baked, or roasted.

For baking or roasting, the skin can be left on. It works as a natural barrier that ensures the carrot retains its flavor and texture. Just be sure to scrub it thoroughly first. You can experiment with different consistencies and preparation methods in the same dish, for example, carrot purée and baked carrot wedges with grated raw carrot topping. You'll have the same vegetable but prepared to be completely different in both taste and texture.

The tops of early carrots can be juiced, sautéed in a skillet and eaten like spinach, or cooked and added to a sauce. Carrots that have gone soft will regain their crispness if you put them in iced water until firm.

STORING
Store carrots in the fridge, preferably in a damp towel. Cut off damaged sections for longer life. Puréed, blanched, or cooked carrots are fine to freeze.

SEASON
Carrots are a cool-weather crop grown in spring and fall. They can be stored in a root vegetable cellar or bought in stores year round.

GOES WELL WITH
Carrots go well with other root vegetables, spinach, lemon, apple, herbs, ginger, saffron, cumin, star anise, seeds, nuts, vinegar, soy, butter, fish, chicken, and lamb.

Carrot with kidney beans, red onion, parsley, and vinaigrette; Carrot with stock and butter; Roasted carrots with garlic. >

22 ways of preparing carrot

RAW
With kidney beans, red onion, parsley, and vinaigrette

Coarsely grate carrots. In a bowl, combine with cooked kidney beans, thinly sliced red onion, and chopped parsley. Whisk together 1 part vinegar, 3 parts olive oil, salt and pepper. Toss the salad in the vinaigrette.

With vinaigrette, cumin, and sunflower seeds

Coarsely grate carrots and place in a bowl. Whisk together 1 part white wine vinegar, 3 parts olive oil, salt and pepper. Add the vinaigrette to the bowl. Season with salt, pepper, and ground cumin, and toss. Sprinkle with roasted sunflower seeds.

With apple, onion, vinaigrette, and sunflower seeds

Coarsely grate carrots and apples into a bowl, combine with finely chopped onion. Whisk together 1 part vinegar, 2 parts oil, salt, and pepper. Toss the salad in the vinaigrette. Sprinkle with sunflower seeds.

With lettuce, onion, orange, vinaigrette, and almonds

Coarsely grate carrots into a bowl. Combine with lettuce leaves and finely chopped onion. Sprinkle with grated orange zest. Whisk together 1 part orange juice, 2 parts olive oil, a dash of white wine vinegar, salt, and pepper. Toss the salad with the vinaigrette. Sprinkle with coarsely chopped, salted almonds.

With red onion, soy, sweet chili, and sesame seeds

Coarsely grate carrots into a bowl. Combine with thinly sliced red onion. Whisk together equal parts soy and chili sauces and add to the bowl. Sprinkle with roasted sesame seeds.

With yogurt, olive oil, garlic, cumin, and chili

Coarsely grate carrots into a bowl. Combine with thick yogurt and olive oil. Add grated garlic and season with ground cumin, chili powder, and salt.

PICKLE
With vinegar, sugar, mustard seeds, and bay leaves

Thinly slice carrots and transfer to a preserving jar. In a pan, boil 1 part vinegar, 2 parts powdered sugar, 3 parts water, mustard seeds, and bay leaves. Pour the hot liquid over the carrots and let sit for at least six hours. Goes well with breaded fish. Can be stored in the fridge for 1–2 weeks.

BOIL
With stock and butter

Chop the carrots. Boil in a saucepan of stock until soft. Drain and blend with butter until you have a smooth purée. Season with salt and pepper. Goes well with oven-roasted meat or with a stew, instead of mashed potatoes.

With butter and parsley or dill

Cut carrots into slices. Boil in a saucepan of salted water until soft. Drain and add a generous pat of butter. Season with chopped parsley or dill, salt, and pepper.

With orange, butter, baby leaf spinach, and tarragon

Cut carrots into equal-sized chunks. Boil in a saucepan of salted water until soft. Drain. Boil orange juice in the same pan. Add a generous pat of butter, baby leaf spinach, and the carrot slices. Season with salt, pepper, and tarragon.

With ginger, butter, and cilantro

Thinly slice carrots. Place in a saucepan with cold water. Bring to the boil and add grated ginger and a generous pat of butter. Boil carrots until soft. Season with salt and pepper and sprinkle with chopped cilantro. Goes well with chicken and fish.

With stock, butter, leek, and parsley

Scrub or peel, then chop carrots. Cover evenly with stock and boil until nearly soft. Add a pat of butter and sliced leeks. Simmer for a few minutes more. Garnish with parsley. Season with salt and pepper.

With onion, garlic, ginger, stock, and crème fraîche

Slice carrots. In a saucepan, fry the slices in oil for a few minutes with chopped onion, garlic, and grated ginger. Cover with stock and cook for 10–15 minutes, or until the carrots are tender. Blend, adding more stock to make a smooth soup. Stir in crème fraîche for a creamier soup. Season with salt and pepper.

FRY
With garlic and parsley

Chop carrots. Sauté in butter with chopped garlic. Season with salt and pepper. Sprinkle with chopped parsley.

With potato

Peel, then coarsely grate carrots and potatoes, and transfer to a bowl. Season with salt and pepper and squeeze out as much of the liquid as possible. Heat the butter and oil in a skillet. Form cakes and fry over a medium heat for about 10 minutes. Flip the cakes over and fry the other side until golden brown. Reduce the heat and cook until done. Goes well with feta or another goat cheese.

With pumpkin seeds and chili

Peel and thinly slice carrots. Sauté in olive oil until soft. Sprinkle with pumpkin seeds, season with chili powder, and simmer for a few more minutes. Season with salt.

ROAST
With garlic, thyme, and cream

Chop carrots and place on a baking tray. Roast at 400 °F (200 °C) for about 15 minutes, or until tender and golden brown. Heat cream with chopped garlic and thyme. Purée carrots, adding more cream until you have a smooth purée. Season with salt and pepper. Goes well with oven-roasted cabbage and goat cheese.

With garlic, cumin, and pumpkin seeds

Peel carrots and halve them lengthwise. Toss in olive oil and crushed garlic, salt, pepper, and ground cumin. Transfer to a baking tray. Roast at 400 °F (200 °C) for about 15 minutes, or until soft and golden brown. Sprinkle with roasted pumpkin seeds.

With lemon, cashews, and soy

Slice carrots and transfer to a baking tray. Toss in olive oil and drizzle with lemon juice. Roast at 400 °F (200 °C) for about 15 minutes, or until soft and golden brown. Combine carrots and roasted cashews in a bowl. Add a dash of light soy sauce. Season with salt and pepper.

With garlic

Scrub carrots, halve lengthwise, and transfer to a baking tray. Toss in olive oil and crushed garlic. Roast at 400 °F (200 °C) for 15 minutes, or until soft and golden brown.

With flavored butter

Scrub carrots thoroughly. Toss in olive oil and transfer to a baking tray. Season with salt and pepper. Roast at 400 °F (200 °C) for about 30 minutes, or until soft and golden brown. Halve the carrots lengthwise and serve with flavored butter (see page 179).

DEEP-FRY
As chips

Thinly slice carrots. Deep-fry in hot oil until golden brown. Drain on paper towels. Season with salt.

RUTABAGA

Rutabaga has much in common with kohlrabi. Its strange appearance can be off-putting to some, but underneath the surprisingly easy-to-peel skin, lies a very delicious root vegetable.

    Some believe that the sweet taste of the rutabaga is too dominant and heavy. However, this can be remedied by either combining it with other flavors, such as butter, potato, or carrot, as in a classic root mash, or by matching it with equally strong flavors, including spicy chili, horseradish, mustard, or vinegar. Rutabaga pickled in vinegar is delicious. Boiling rutabaga until soft, but still with a little "bite," also reduces the sweetness. Rutabaga is less sweet raw, grated, or fried than boiled, with a flavor comparable to that of carrot. It's also worth knowing that the older the rutabaga, the more intense its flavor, so choose young roots if you prefer a milder taste.

    Rutabaga is available in many variations and colors. Even under the skin, they range from white to true golden yellow, and the colors are also retained during cooking. Rutabaga that has turned soft will regain its firmness if you place it in iced water.

STORING
Store rutabaga in the fridge, preferably in a damp towel. Puréed and parboiled rutabaga can be frozen.

SEASON
Planted in late spring after any danger of frost, rutabaga is harvested in fall.

GOES WELL WITH
Rutabaga goes well with, for example, pork, potatoes, carrots, butter, lemon, kale, parsley, apples, mustard, horseradish, honey, ginger, chili, and other root vegetables.

12 ways of preparing rutabaga

RAW

With kale, red onion, mustard, and vinaigrette

Peel and coarsely grate rutabaga. In a bowl, combine the rutabaga with thinly shredded blanched or raw kale and sliced red onion. Whisk together 1 part Dijon mustard, 1 part red wine vinegar, 3 parts oil, salt, and pepper. Add the vinaigrette to the bowl.

With parsley, orange, honey, goat cheese, and pumpkin seeds

Peel and shred rutabaga. In a bowl, combine the rutabaga with chopped parsley. Whisk together 1 part orange juice, 2 parts olive oil, grated orange zest, honey, salt, and pepper. Add to the bowl. Crumble over goat cheese and sprinkle with roasted pumpkin seeds.

BOIL

With carrot, yellow onion, butter, and parsley

Peel and cut rutabaga and carrots into strips and onion into wedges. Boil in a saucepan of salted water with a pat of butter for about 10 minutes or until soft. Drain, lightly season with salt and pepper, then add butter and chopped parsley.

With butter, ginger, and orange

Peel rutabaga and cut into small cubes. Boil in a saucepan of salted water until soft. Drain. Stir in a pat of butter. Season with finely chopped ginger, freshly squeezed orange juice, salt, and pepper. Goes well with, for example, chicken or fish.

With potato, butter, and parsley

Peel and chop rutabaga and potatoes. Boil in a pan of salted water until soft. Mash roughly with a potato masher and mix in the butter. Season with chopped parsley, salt, and pepper.

With kale, leek, lemon dressing, and horseradish

Peel rutabaga and cut into wedges. Boil in a pan of salted water until soft. Add shredded kale and simmer for 30 seconds. Drain. Place in a bowl along with thinly sliced leek. Whisk together 1 part lemon juice, 2 parts olive oil, salt, and pepper. Stir the dressing into the bowl and add some shredded horseradish. Goes well with fish.

FRY

With carrot, potato, thyme, onion, and parsley

Peel rutabaga, carrots, and potatoes, and cut into small cubes. Coarsely chop onions. Fry the root vegetables in oil and butter with a sprig of thyme until soft. Add the onion at the end of the cooking time. Season with salt and pepper, and sprinkle with chopped parsley.

With apple, almonds, and parsley

Peel rutabaga and cut into thin wedges. Boil in a saucepan of salted water over a high heat. Drain. Fry rutabaga and sliced apple in butter. Season with salt and pepper, sprinkle with chopped almonds and parsley.

With ginger, lemon, and honey

Peel and chop rutabaga. Boil in a saucepan of salted water until soft. Drain. Fry the rutabaga in butter until golden brown. Add chopped ginger and grated lemon zest, and drizzle with honey. Fry for a few more minutes while stirring. Season with salt and pepper.

ROAST

With root vegetables, onion, garlic, and thyme

Peel and chop rutabaga and other root vegetables. Put on a baking tray and turn in olive oil, salt, pepper, chopped onion, and whole garlic cloves. Roast at 400°F (200°C) for about 20 minutes, or until soft. Sprinkle with thyme. Goes well with most dishes.

With dill, vinegar, sugar, yellow onion, and mustard seeds

Place thin rutabaga slices and a few dill stems in a jar with a lid. Boil 1 part vinegar, 2 parts sugar, 3 parts water, sliced onions, mustard seeds and dill seeds. Pour the hot liquid over the rutabaga, cover with the lid and let stand for a few hours. Can be stored in the fridge for up to one month.

With vinegar, sugar, chili, and ginger

Dice and cook rutabaga in salted water until almost soft. Drain. Place in a jar with a lid. Boil 1 part vinegar, 2 parts powdered sugar, 3 parts water, sliced chili, and ginger. Pour the hot liquid over the rutabaga, cover with the lid, and let stand for one day. Can be stored in the fridge for up to three months.

PARSNIP

The parsnip is, after celery root and parsley root, the root that needs the longest time to ripen. It looks like parsley root, but parsnips usually grow longer and thicker than parsley roots. And, of course, they also differ greatly in taste.

It is hard to believe that what looks like a tough, white root hides deep, sweet, and earthy flavors that unfold fully when it is cooked. The parsnip's flavor can be quite dominant. An easy trick is to cook it with other root vegetables, or to counteract its earthiness with a dash of cream, milk, or butter. A few drops of lemon juice or vinegar will neutralize excessive sweetness. Be aware that parsnips become sweeter the longer they are cooked.

Small cubes of parsnip can be fried in a pan or roasted, but be careful as it burns easily. If you prefer larger chunks, it's a good idea to parboil them for a couple of minutes in salted water before frying.

You can leave the skin on if you roast a parsnip whole in the oven; it ensures it will retain both flavor and texture. Just make sure to scrub the skin thoroughly before cooking. Thanks to their high sugar content, parsnips can be pickled and work well when preserved with carrots and ginger.

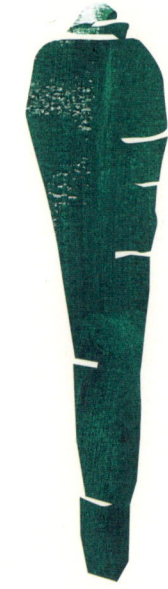

STORING
Store parsnips in the fridge, preferably in a damp towel. Puréed, parboiled, or cooked parsnips are fine to freeze.

SEASON
Parsnips are a cool-weather crop with a long growing season, and are started in the garden early in the spring before the last frost, or in the fall. They can withstand cold and can overwinter in the ground. Parsnips store well and are available in stores well into late winter.

GOES WELL WITH
Parsnip goes well with other root vegetables, garlic, herbs, lemon, apple, orange, honey, saffron, vinegar, cream, butter, and pork.

Parsnip with pork sausage, apple, and parsley. >

21 ways of preparing parsnip

BOIL

With milk, butter, and lemon

Peel and chop parsnips and place in a saucepan. Cover with milk and boil until soft. Drain the milk and reserve. Blend the parsnips to a purée. Dilute with some of the milk to the desired consistency. Stir in butter and season with grated lemon zest, lemon juice, grated garlic, salt, and pepper. Goes well with chicken.

With butter, watercress, and vinegar

Peel and chop parsnips. Boil in salted water until soft. Drain and add butter and a generous handful of watercress. Drizzle with vinegar, season with salt and pepper, and toss to combine. Goes well with fish.

With potato

Add boiled parsnips to potatoes when you are preparing your regular mash.

With potato, butter, dill or parsley, and lemon

Peel 1 part parsnips and 2 parts potatoes and cut into small chunks. Boil in a saucepan of salted water until soft. Drain and add a generous pat of butter. Mash roughly with a potato masher. Stir in plenty of chopped dill or parsley. Season the purée with lemon juice, salt, and pepper.

With potato, yellow onion, apple, stock, cream, and mustard

Peel equal parts of parsnips and potatoes and cut into cubes. Sauté in a skillet with oil, chopped onion, and cubed apples. Cover with stock and cook until soft. Blend, adding more stock and cream to make a smooth soup. Season with Dijon mustard, salt, and pepper.

With leek, garlic, tomato, and dill

Peel the parsnips and cut into medallions. Boil in a saucepan of salted water until soft. Drain. Fry thinly sliced leeks and garlic in butter until soft but do not allow to brown. Add parsnips, chopped tomatoes, and more butter. Cook for a few minutes more. Season with salt and pepper, sprinkle with chopped dill. Goes well with fish.

With potato, béchamel sauce, and mustard

Peel and chop parsnips and potatoes. Boil in a saucepan of salted water until soft. Drain and add the béchamel sauce. Flavor with Dijon mustard. Goes well with sausages.

In soups or stews

Chop parsnips and cook in soups or stews.

FRY

With garlic, hazelnuts, and parsley

Peel parsnips and cut into thin slices. Fry in oil until soft and golden brown. Add finely chopped garlic and cook for a few more minutes. Transfer to a plate, sprinkle with coarsely chopped hazelnuts and a generous handful of chopped parsley. Goes with fried kale.

With apple cider vinegar

Peel and chop parsnips and potatoes. Sauté in oil until soft and golden brown. Drizzle with apple cider vinegar and season with salt.

With thyme and sunflower seeds

Peel and chop parsnips. Boil in a pan of salted water until soft, then drain. Brown a generous pat of butter with thyme in a skillet. Add the parsnips and sauté until golden brown. Season with salt and pepper, and sprinkle with roasted sunflower seeds.

With potato, garlic, apple, almonds, and parsley or spinach

Peel parsnips and cut into small cubes. Boil in a saucepan of salted water until soft. Drain. In a skillet, sauté the parsnips in olive oil and butter until golden brown. Add finely chopped garlic and sliced apple, and cook for a few minutes more. Season with salt and pepper. Sprinkle with roasted flaked almonds and add finely chopped parsley or spinach.

With potato, mushrooms, garlic, and cream

Peel and chop parsnips and potatoes. Fry until soft and golden brown. Add sliced mushrooms and sauté until soft. Add chopped garlic, salt, and pepper. Pour in a dash of cream and bring to the boil. Goes well with burgers.

With pork sausage, apple, and parsley

Peel and slice parsnips. Boil in a saucepan of salted water until soft. Halve a smoked pork sausage lengthwise and peel off the skin. Fry in a pat of butter until crispy. Add the parsnip slices and fry for a few minutes. Season with salt and pepper, add grated apple, and sprinkle with plenty of chopped parsley.

ROAST
With root vegetables

Peel and chop parsnips and other root vegetables. Place in an ovenproof dish with olive oil, salt, and pepper. Roast at 400°F (200°C) for about 20 minutes, or until soft and golden brown. Serve on its own or add to regular potato purée.

With lemon dressing, garlic, and parsley

Peel and chop parsnips. Place in an ovenproof dish with olive oil, salt, and pepper. Roast at 400°F (200°C) for 20 minutes, or until soft. In a bowl, whisk together 1 part lemon juice, 2 parts olive oil, crushed garlic, chopped parsley, salt, and pepper. Turn the parsnips in the lemon dressing.

With potato, garlic, rosemary, and goat cheese

Peel and chop parsnips and potatoes. Place in an ovenproof dish with olive oil, crushed garlic, and some rosemary sprigs. Roast at 400°F (200°C) for 20 minutes, or until soft and golden brown. Crumble over goat cheese. Goes well with, for example, lamb.

With yellow onion, thyme, and walnuts

Peel and chop parsnips and yellow onion. Place in an ovenproof dish with olive oil, thyme, salt, and pepper. Roast at 400°F (200°C) for about 20 minutes, or until soft and golden brown. Add chopped walnuts just before serving.

With mayonnaise, garlic and saffron

Peel and chop parsnips into coarse chunks. Place in an ovenproof dish with olive oil, grated garlic, salt, and pepper and roast for 20 minutes at 400°F (200°C), or until soft and golden brown. Mix the mayonnaise (see p. 177) with crushed garlic and saffron. Serve with the parsnips.

DEEP-FRY
As chips

Cut parsnips into very thin slices. Deep-fry in hot oil until golden brown, drain on paper towels. Season with salt.

As a topping

Coarsely grate parsnips with a grater. Deep-fry until golden brown and drain on paper towels. Sprinkle over salads, fish, or parsnip purée.

See also the parsley root tips on page 78.

PARSLEY ROOT

At first glance, the white and conical parsley root looks very similar to the better-known parsnip. However, parsley root is smaller as well as thinner than parsnip. And if you smell the roots, it's quite easy to tell them apart: parsnips have an earthy and sweet scent while parsley roots are fresh and aromatic.

Although many people love parsley roots, it's not usually a gardener's favorite vegetable. One reason is that it needs such a long time to ripen. There is also less demand for parsley root compared to other more widely known root vegetables, such as carrots and beets.

Even though parsley root has an aroma reminiscent of parsley, its taste is actually closer to that of celery root. It can be eaten raw, but its true flavors are only released when it is cooked.

Parsley root works well with other root vegetables in fall stews and soups, as well as fried, deep-fried, or oven-roasted. The skin can be left on as this natural barrier helps retain both taste and texture. Just scrub it properly first. The leaves can also be eaten. Their taste is similar to leaf parsley but stronger and slightly more bitter.

STORING
Store parsley roots in the fridge, preferably in a damp towel. Puréed, blanched, or cooked parsley root freezes well.

SEASON
Parsley root is a difficult crop to cultivate and requires consistently cool temperatures. In all but the mildest climates, it is grown in fall or early spring.

GOES WELL WITH
Parsley root goes well with, for example, other root vegetables, herbs, garlic, lemon, and honey.

Parsley root with yellow onion, garlic, stock, vinegar, and thyme. >

11 ways of preparing parsley root

BOIL

With milk and butter
Peel and chop parsley root. Boil in a saucepan of milk until soft. Drain the milk and reserve. Stir a pat of butter into the parsley root and mash. Dilute with milk to make a smooth purée. Season with salt and pepper.

With butter and dill or parsley
Peel and chop parsley root. Boil in a saucepan of salted water until soft. Drain, add a pat of butter and mash roughly with a potato masher. Stir in chopped dill or parsley. Season with salt and pepper. Goes well with fish.

With butter, parsley, and lemon
Peel and chop parsley root. Boil in a saucepan of salted water until soft. Drain and add a pat of butter and plenty of chopped parsley. Season with lemon juice, salt, and pepper.

With butter, tomato, and spinach
Peel and chop parsley root. Boil in a saucepan of salted water until soft. Drain and add a pat of butter, halved cherry tomatoes, and grated spinach. Season with salt and pepper. Goes well with roast chicken.

With yellow onion, garlic, stock, vinegar, and thyme
Peel and chop parsley root. Fry in a skillet with olive oil, chopped onion, and garlic until soft. Cover with stock and dilute with more stock to make a soup. Flavor with white wine vinegar, thyme, salt, and pepper.

FRY

With leek and kale or Tuscan cabbage
Peel parsley root and cut into thin slices. Fry in a pan with oil until soft and golden brown. Add thinly sliced leeks and shredded kale or Tuscan cabbage, and fry for a few more minutes. Season with salt and pepper.

With lemon and parsley
Peel and chop parsley root. Boil in a pan with salted water and squeezed lemon juice. Drain. Fry in butter until golden brown. Season with salt and pepper, and sprinkle with parsley.

With mushrooms, garlic, red onion, parsley, and cheese
Peel parsley root and cut into wedges. Boil in a saucepan of salted water until soft. Drain. Fry mushrooms and crushed garlic in olive oil and butter for a few minutes. Add sliced red onion and the parsley root slices and fry until golden brown. Season with salt and pepper, and garnish with chopped parsley. Top with grated Parmesan or another hard cheese.

ROAST

With lemon
Peel and chop parsley root. Place on a baking tray with oil, salt, and pepper. Roast at 400 °F (200 °C) for 15–20 minutes, or until soft and golden brown. Season with grated lemon zest.

With shallot and garlic
Peel and chop parsley root and shallots. Place on a baking tray with oil, finely chopped garlic, salt, and pepper. Roast at 400 °F (200 °C) for about 15–20 minutes, or until soft and golden brown.

DEEP-FRY

As chips
Cut parsley root into very thin slices. Rinse in iced water and drain well. When the slices are completely dry, deep-fry them in hot oil until golden brown. Drain on paper towels. Season with salt.

See also the parsnip tips on page 74–75.

SWEET POTATO

Despite their robust appearance, sweet potatoes have a fairly thin skin, which means that they have a short shelf life. The color of the skin varies—mostly, it is red or light brown, and underneath the flesh is white, yellow, or orange. Sweet potatoes are starchy like regular potatoes, but much sweeter, as the name indicates.

Peel sweet potatoes and boil them in salted water or stock. Mash them coarsely and season with butter, garlic, and chili, or mash and thin with stock to make a purée or a soup. Cut sweet potatoes into small cubes or thin slices, and fry them in a skillet. Larger chunks should be parboiled, then roasted until soft and golden brown. Sweet potato fries or sweet potato chips are a deliciously different treat. Serve with a sour cream dip.

Sweet potatoes can be added to pies and gratins and, thanks to their sweetness, they can also be used in pastries and desserts.

STORING
Store at room temperature in a cool, dry, well-ventilated spot. Puréed sweet potato can be frozen.

SEASON
Organic sweet potatoes can be harvested all year round.

GOES WELL WITH
Sweet potatoes go well with, for example, spinach, chili, garlic, ginger, black beans, cumin, cayenne pepper, nuts, sausages, chicken, pork, and lamb.

13 ways of preparing sweet potato

BOIL

With stock, butter, garlic, and hot chili paste

Peel and chop sweet potatoes. Boil in vegetable stock until soft. Drain and reserve some of the stock. Mash the sweet potatoes with a little stock and a pat of butter using a potato masher. Season with crushed garlic, hot chili paste, salt, and black pepper. Goes well with, for example, spicy sausages or lamb.

With potato, butter, garlic, cumin, and chili

Peel equal parts sweet potatoes and potatoes and cut into cubes. Boil in a saucepan of salted water until soft. Drain. Add butter and olive oil, and mash with a potato masher. Season with grated garlic, cumin, chili, salt, and pepper. Goes well with pork or chicken.

FRY

With garlic, chili, and spinach or chard

Peel sweet potatoes and cut into small cubes. Fry in oil with crushed garlic and sliced chili until soft and golden brown. Season with salt and pepper. Add shredded spinach or chard.

ROAST

With butter, garlic, lemon, and parsley

Scrub whole sweet potatoes and prick a few holes in the skin with a fork. Roast at 350 °F (175 °C) for 40 minutes, or until soft. Season softened butter with crushed garlic, lemon juice, chopped parsley, salt, and pepper. Serve with the sweet potatoes.

With garlic and Parmesan

Peel and chop sweet potatoes. Place in an ovenproof dish with olive oil, crushed garlic, salt, and pepper. Roast at 400 °F (200 °C) for about 15–20 minutes, or until soft and golden brown. Top with grated Parmesan cheese.

With onion, garlic, spinach, and cashews

Peel sweet potatoes and cut into cubes. Place on a baking tray with olive oil, chopped onion, chopped garlic, salt, and pepper. Roast at 400 °F (200 °C) for about 20 minutes, or until soft and golden brown. Add finely chopped spinach and roasted cashew nuts. Goes well with, for example, lamb or chicken.

With butter and chili

Put oven-roasted sweet potatoes into a bowl. Add a pat of butter and mash. Season with salt, pepper, and chopped chili.

With ginger, lemon, and olive oil

Halve oven-roasted sweet potatoes and scoop out the flesh. Mash with a potato masher. Season with crushed ginger, lemon juice, olive oil, and salt. Goes well with, for example, chicken.

With almonds, chili, and cilantro

In a bowl, combine blanched almonds, finely chopped chili, and plenty of chopped cilantro. Sprinkle over oven-roasted sweet potato.

With yogurt, hot chili paste, and lemon

Flavor thick yogurt with hot chili paste, lemon juice and salt. Serve with oven-roasted sweet potatoes.

With cream cheese, lemon, and chive

Season cream cheese with lemon juice, finely chopped chives, salt, and pepper. Serve with oven-roasted sweet potatoes.

With butter and hot chili paste

In a bowl, stir together softened butter and hot chili paste. Serve with oven-roasted sweet potatoes.

DEEP-FRY

As chips

Cut sweet potatoes into thin strips. Deep-fry in hot oil until golden brown, drain on paper towels. Season with salt.

< Sweet potatoes with butter, garlic, lemon, and parsley.

RADISH AND BLACK RADISH

Red radishes are enjoyed for many reasons: they are easy to cultivate, grow quickly, and are simple to prepare. Radishes are delicious raw with a sprinkling of salt or a little butter or cream cheese. They come in many shapes, sizes, and colors, but all have the same characteristic peppery flavor. The main difference between red and the larger black radishes is that black radish has a stronger mustard flavor. It's also harder and can be stored over winter in a cool, dark room. By comparison, red radishes tend to become wrinkly and dry out quickly if they are not eaten shortly after being harvested.

Red radishes are usually eaten raw, either whole or sliced into salads. Very peppery varieties can be grated into sauces instead of horseradish. Boil radishes until soft in salted water, then toss them in butter with other fresh vegetables. Frying or baking with new potatoes works well, although cooked radishes lose some flavor and color.

Black radishes are usually associated with Asian food, and are often marinated together with herbs and spices for noodle soups or wok dishes. Grate or slice very thinly and add to salads or sandwiches, or serve with salt, pepper, oil, and vinegar.

Milder varieties of black radish can also be cooked or fried. **Daikon** is a juicy and sweet, white-skinned, long, tapered Japanese radish.

STORING
Radishes are best stored in a damped towel in the fridge. If necessary, cut off the leaves to help preserve them. Radishes are not suitable for freezing.

SEASON
This easy-to-grow crop is planted in spring and fall, and harvested during early summer or late fall. It is available year-round in stores.

GOES WELL WITH
Radishes go well with, for example, potatoes, asparagus, carrots, cucumber, beans, butter, lemon, vinaigrette, lime, soy, sesame, and oil.

Radishes and leaves with butter. >

20 ways of preparing radish & black radish

RAW

Radishes with salt or cream cheese, lemon, and chive

Dip freshly picked red radishes in salt or cream cheese flavored with grated lemon zest and chopped chives.

Radishes with fish

In fish dishes, replace horseradish with grated radishes. Watch your fingertips when grating!

Radishes with rye bread, cream cheese, parsley, and lemon

Cut rye bread into fingers. Put them onto a baking tray and bake at 300 °F (150 °C), until toasted. Process the toast into breadcrumbs in a blender. Mix cream cheese and chopped parsley to a smooth cream. Season with salt, pepper, and lemon juice. Dip the radishes in cream cheese and breadcrumbs.

Radishes with green or potato salad

Cut radishes into very thin slices. Place in iced water for a few minutes. Drain. Add to green or potato salads.

Radishes with onion, cress, and vinaigrette

Cut radishes into very thin slices. Place in iced water for a few minutes. Pour off the water and drain. Combine with sliced onion and cress. Whisk together 1 part vinegar and 3 parts olive oil, salt, and pepper. Add the vinaigrette to the bowl and stir to combine.

Radishes with avocado, onion, green chili, lime, and cilantro

Cut radishes into very thin slices. Place in iced water for a few minutes. Drain. In a bowl, combine with sliced avocado, chopped onion, and chili. Flavor with squeezed lime juice, grated lime zest, and salt. Drizzle with olive oil and sprinkle with chopped cilantro. Goes well with, for example, broiled fish.

Radishes with fennel, lettuce, and vinaigrette

Cut radishes and fennel into very thin slices. Place in iced water for a few minutes. Drain. In a bowl, combine with torn lettuce leaves. Whisk together 1 part vinegar and 3 parts olive oil, salt, and pepper. Stir the vinaigrette into the bowl.

Black radish with cucumber and lemon dressing

Peel black radish and cucumber and cut into thin slices. Place in a bowl. Whisk together 1 part lemon juice, 2 parts olive oil, salt, and pepper. Add the dressing to the bowl. Goes well with, for example, mussels and shrimp.

Radishes/black radish with mayonnaise, soy, and dried red pepper flakes

Flavor mayonnaise with light soy sauce and/or dried red pepper flakes. Dip radish or black radish strips into the mayonnaise.

Black radish with carrot, cucumber, leek, red pepper, ginger, lemon, and rice paper

Cut black radish, carrots, cucumber, and leek into thin strips. Place in a bowl and season with dried red pepper flakes, finely chopped ginger, lemon juice, and salt. Soak sheets of rice paper in warm water for a couple of seconds. Place the vegetables on top and roll up. Dip the spring rolls in light soy sauce mixed with wasabi, sweet chili, or teriyaki sauce.

Black radish with carrot, scallion, soy, wasabi, ginger, and seaweed

Peel black radish and carrots and cut into strips. Mix with sliced scallion in a bowl. Whisk light soy sauce with a little wasabi and chopped ginger. Add to the bowl with torn seaweed leaves. Goes well with, for example, fish, shrimp, or noodles.

Radishes with sugar peas, herbs, and lemon dressing

In a bowl, combine halved radishes with sliced sugar peas, and chopped herbs of your choice. Whisk together 1 part lemon juice, 2 parts olive oil, salt, and pepper. Add the dressing to the bowl and stir to combine. Goes well with, for example, steamed fish.

PICKLE
Black Radish with sugar, vinegar, green onion, chili, and ginger

Whisk together 1 part powdered sugar, 1 part vinegar, 1 part water, and some salt. Place shredded black radish in a preserving jar with a lid. Cover with the liquid and let stand for at least 30 minutes. Remove the horseradish. Combine in a bowl with sliced scallion, chili, and diced ginger. Goes well with, for example, salmon. Can be stored in the fridge for about one week. Black radish loses its firmness the longer it is marinated in vinegar.

BOIL
Radishes with root vegetables, butter, and dill

Boil radishes and other vegetables, such as onions, carrots, asparagus, and potatoes, in separate saucepans of salted water. Drain and mix in a bowl. Add a pat of butter and chopped dill. Season with salt and pepper.

Radishes with peas, butter, dill, and lemon

Boil garden peas in a saucepan of salted water until soft. Pour off the water; add a pat of butter, halved radishes, and plenty of chopped dill. Season with salt, pepper, and lemon juice.

Black Radish with carrot and leek

Peel black radish and carrots. Cut radish, carrots, and leek into really thin, long noodle strips, preferably with a mandolin slicer. Add to the wok at the end of the cooking time and warm through.

FRY
Black Radish with carrot, leek, garlic, and spinach

Cut black radish, carrots, and leek into thin strips. In a skillet, sauté finely chopped garlic in olive oil but don't allow it to brown. Add the vegetables and fry in the garlic oil for a minute. Stir in torn spinach leaves and briefly let them soften. Season with salt and pepper. Goes well with fish.

Radishes with cucumber, red onion, and spinach

Chop radishes. Quickly fry them in butter and oil along with peeled and diced cucumber and sliced red onion. Add torn spinach leaves and cook until softened. Season with salt and pepper. Goes well with, for example, fish.

Leaves of radishes with butter

Radish leaves can also be eaten. Remove any tough or yellow leaves and sauté the remaining leaves in butter in a skillet. Season with salt and pepper.

ROAST
Radishes with potato and onion

Place radishes, potatoes, chopped onion, and olive oil on a baking tray. Season with salt and pepper. Roast at 400 °F (200 °C) for 20 minutes, or until soft.

CRISPY
Radish slices will be even crispier, and wrinkly radishes can be revived, if briefly placed in iced water before serving.

BEET

The first small beets are harvested in early summer and are often sold in little bundles. They are juicy and crunchy, and the flavor is relatively light and spicy. Early beets are delicious no matter how they are cooked, and they are also very tasty thinly sliced and enjoyed raw. Boil beets with the skin on and with 1 inch (2.5 cm) of the root tip remaining, otherwise they will lose both color and taste. Also keep the skin on when oven-roasting whole beets, to retain their flavor. Fresh beet leaves can be used in the same way as spinach and chard.

Late varieties arrive in the fall. The extra weeks they spent in the soil not only concentrate the sweet, earthy taste of beets, but also increase their nutritional value. Late varieties are slightly drier in texture and have a thicker skin. As they are larger, they are perfect for pickling in vinegar or adding to warming soups and stews, as well as, of course, boiled and oven-roasted. Boil some extra beets when you are cooking, drain, and place in a bowl in the fridge to use in salads the following day, or to roast in the oven. If you want to combine raw beets with other salad vegetables, grate or thinly slice them and place the slices in cold water to enhance their chunky texture. The sweetness of beets increases with cooking; it can be offset by lemon juice or vinegar.

STORING
Store beets in the fridge, preferably in a damp towel. Puréed, parboiled, or cooked beets are fine to freeze.

SEASON
Organic beets can be harvested from early summer to early fall. Beets for storage are harvested from high summer to late fall. Available to buy well into late winter.

GOES WELL WITH
Beets go well with, for instance, kale, horseradish, lemon, rosemary, parsley, dill, capers, balsamic vinegar, honey, roasted pine nuts, Parmesan cheese, goat cheese, feta cheese, butter, fish, and lamb.

< Beet with butter, capers, dill or parsley.

> Yellow beets and Chioggia beets can be used in all beet recipes, as they are close in flavor. Chioggia beet are attractive, but unfortunately the beautiful red-white color disappears during cooking. White beet is the sweetest of all beets.

36 ways of preparing beet

RAW

With arugula or baby leaf spinach, vinaigrette, and walnuts

Peel and coarsely grate beets. Place in a bowl with arugula or baby leaf spinach. In a bowl, whisk together 1 part balsamic vinegar, 3 parts olive oil, salt, and pepper. Stir the vinaigrette into the bowl. Sprinkle with chopped walnuts.

In a salad or with olive oil and lemon

Peel beets and cut into very thin slices, preferably with a mandolin slicer. Place in iced water for a few minutes. Drain. Add the slices to a salad or place a few slices on a plate and drizzle with olive oil and lemon. Season with salt and pepper.

With arugula and pesto

Peel beets and cut into very thin slices, preferably with a mandolin slicer. In a bowl, combine the sliced beets with arugula and stir in pesto. Season with salt and pepper.

PICKLE

With vinegar, sugar, dill seeds, and mustard seeds

Peel beets and cut into very thin slices, preferably with a mandolin slicer. Put into a preserving jar with a lid. In a saucepan, boil 1 part vinegar, 2 parts powdered sugar, 3 parts water, dill seeds, mustard seeds, and a little salt. Cover the beets with the hot liquid, close the lid, and set aside for at least a couple of hours. Goes well with, for example, pies and rillettes. Pickled beets can be stored in the fridge for up to one month.

With vinegar, sugar, and star anise

In a saucepan of salted water, boil whole beets until soft. Pour off the water and let cool slightly. Peel and cut into wedges and place in a jar with a lid. Boil 1 part vinegar, 2 parts powdered sugar, and 3 parts water in the saucepan. Cover the beets with the hot liquid, close the lid, and set aside for at least one day. Goes well with, for example, butter-fried fish with capers, casseroles, or smoked pork sausages. Can be stored in the fridge for up to three months.

With butter, capers, dill, or parsley

Cut pickled beets into even-sized cubes. In a bowl, turn the beets in melted butter along with capers and finely chopped dill or parsley. Season with pepper. Goes well with butter-fried fish or burgers.

With gherkin, apple, and sour cream

Cut pickled beets into cubes. Mix with chopped gherkins and diced apple. Add sour cream. Season with salt and pepper. Goes well with breaded fish.

BOIL

Boil whole

Boil whole unpeeled beets in a saucepan of salted water for 20–50 minutes, or until soft. Peel the beets while warm. Serve with one of the suggestions for hot beets on page 90.

With bacon, lettuce, red onion, vinaigrette, and goat cheese

Slice freshly cooked beets. In a bowl, combine them with crispy fried smoked bacon, torn lettuce leaves, and finely chopped red onion. Whisk together 1 part balsamic vinegar, 3 parts olive oil, salt, and pepper. Add the vinaigrette to the bowl and stir to combine. Top with crumbled goat cheese.

With butter, capers, herbs, and spinach or arugula

Slice freshly cooked beets. Melt or brown butter in a skillet. Add the beets, capers, salt, and pepper, and sprinkle with herbs, such as chives, dill, parsley, cress, and spinach or arugula.

With lemon dressing, honey, and thyme

Thinly slice freshly cooked beets and place on a platter. Whisk together 1 part lemon juice, 2 parts olive oil, honey, salt, and pepper. Pour the dressing over the beets. Sprinkle with thyme.

With vinaigrette, pine nuts, and Parmesan

Cut hot or cold cooked beets into thin slices and place in a bowl. Whisk together 1 part vinegar, 3 parts olive oil, salt, and pepper. Pour over the beets. Sprinkle with roasted pine nuts and top with grated Parmesan cheese.

With vinaigrette, Pecorino, sunflower seeds, and parsley

Cut hot or cold cooked beets into slices and place in a bowl. Whisk together 1 part apple cider vinegar, 3 parts cold-pressed rapeseed oil, salt, and pepper. Pour the vinaigrette over the beets, add grated Pecorino cheese, and sprinkle with roasted sunflower seeds and chopped parsley.

With red onion, apple, mayonnaise, and lemon

Cut cold cooked beets into slices. In a bowl, mix with finely chopped red onion, diced apple, and mayonnaise. Flavor with grated lemon zest, a few drops of lemon juice, salt, and pepper. Goes well with ham and whole grain mustard.

With leek, dill, and lemon dressing

Cut cold cooked beets into slices. In a bowl, combine the beets with thinly sliced leek and chopped dill. Whisk together 1 part lemon juice, 2 parts olive oil, salt, and pepper. Stir the dressing into the bowl.

With stock and red chili

Peel and coarsely grate beets. Boil vegetable stock and chopped chili in a saucepan. Add the beets and simmer gently in the stock for about 10 minutes until soft. Drain and season with salt and pepper.

FRY
With feta or Roquefort and walnuts

Peel and coarsely grate beets. Squeeze out as much of the liquid as possible. Put the mixture into a bowl. Season with salt and pepper. Form into cakes. Fry in butter until crispy on both sides. Top with crumbled feta or Roquefort cheese and sprinkle with chopped walnuts.

With Jerusalem artichoke and/or potato

Peel beets, Jerusalem artichokes, and/or potatoes and coarsely grate. Squeeze out as much of the liquid as possible. Put the mixture into a bowl. Season with salt and pepper. Shape into a thin pancake. Heat butter and oil in a skillet, add the pancake, and fry over a medium heat for about 5 minutes. Turn the pancake over and continue until it has browned.

With red onion, chard or spinach, pine nuts, and Parmesan

Peel beets and cut into thin slices. Fry with thin slices of red onion in olive oil until soft. Fold in torn chard or spinach leaves and fry for a few more minutes. Season with salt and pepper. Sprinkle with roasted pine nuts and grated Parmesan cheese.

With bacon, Parmesan, and basil

Cut cold cooked beets into thin slices. Fry in butter together with chopped bacon. Add grated Parmesan cheese and stir in finely chopped basil leaves.

With yellow wax beans, leek, and capers

Chop cold cooked beets. Fry over a high heat in olive oil along with yellow wax beans and thinly sliced leek. Stir in the capers. Season with salt and pepper. Goes well with fish.

With lamb and goat cheese

Roughly grate cold cooked beets. Combine with ground lamb and crumbled goat cheese. Shape the mixture into burgers and fry in olive oil until golden and crispy.

ROAST

Whole

Thoroughly scrub whole small beets. Put the beets on a baking tray and drizzle with olive oil. Roast at 325 °F (175 °C) until soft. Halve the beets or cut into wedges and serve with one of the suggestions in the next column.

With halloumi and oil

Peel beets and cut into wedges. Put on a baking tray, add olive oil, salt, and pepper. Roast at 400 °F (200 °C) for 20–30 minutes, or until soft. Top with cubed halloumi cheese toward the end of the cooking time. Drizzle with olive oil.

With oregano or thyme

Peel beets and cut into wedges. In a bowl, mix olive oil, oregano or thyme, salt, and pepper. Spread evenly on pieces of aluminum foil, place beets on top, and fold into parcels. Roast at 400 °F (200 °C) for about 30 minutes, or until soft.

BAKE

In wholemeal bread

Mix coarsely grated beets into the dough when baking wholemeal bread.

DEEP-FRY

As chips

Cut beets into very thin slices. Rinse in iced water and drain well. When they are completely dry, deep-fry in hot oil until golden brown and drain on paper towels. Season with salt.

BBQ

Whole with butter

Scrub whole small beets. Place on a piece of aluminum foil, fold over and put directly onto the charcoal. Cook until soft. Halve the beets and serve with one of the suggestions in the next column.

HOT BEET SERVING IDEAS

With butter and lemon

Flavor softened butter with grated lemon zest, lemon juice, salt, and pepper.

With butter, lemon, garlic, and herbs

Flavor softened butter with lemon juice, crushed garlic, chopped herbs, salt, and pepper.

With butter and goat cheese

Stir together equal parts of softened butter and goat cheese. Season with salt and pepper.

With Roquefort and crème fraîche

Mix Roquefort cheese and a little crème fraîche. Season with pepper.

With mayonnaise, mustard, and lemon

Flavor mayonnaise with Dijon mustard, lemon juice, salt, and pepper.

With cream cheese and horseradish

Flavor cream cheese with grated horseradish, salt, and pepper.

With honey, rosemary, and goat cheese

Stir finely chopped rosemary into honey. Pour the mixture over hot beets and crumble over goat cheese. Season with salt and pepper.

With vinaigrette, honey, and walnuts

In a bowl, whisk together 1 part vinegar, 3 parts olive oil, some honey, salt, and pepper. Pour the vinaigrette over the beets and sprinkle with roasted walnuts.

BLACK SALSIFY

Black salsify is easily forgotten as a vegetable, but its robust skin hides a delicacy whose taste is similar to that of asparagus. Peeling it can be a little tricky and, above all, sticky. Peel it under running water, then put it immediately into a bowl of water with a little lemon juice as the flesh easily oxidizes and turns brown. Use the lemon water to freshen your hands after peeling.

There are at least two good reasons not to eat raw black salsify. In common with Jerusalem artichokes, they contain inulin, which can cause gassiness. They also taste a thousand times better when cooked. Cut peeled black salsify into small cubes and boil in salted water or stock until soft. Salsify goes well with browned butter, gremolata (finely chopped garlic, lemon zest, parsley, and olive oil) or hollandaise sauce. Creamy black salsify is best prepared by first boiling in salted water until soft, then folding in the hot cream. Or chop and boil together with other vegetables until soft for a soup or stew.

You can also fry black salsify. Just make sure the slices are thin so they cook before burning. You can blanch them which speeds up the process. If you roast them uncooked in the oven, start at 300°F (150°C) until they are soft, then increase to 400°F (200°C) and allow to brown. A creamy gratin made from black salsify, potatoes, and garlic goes well with game and beef.

STORING
Black salsify is best stored wrapped in a kitchen towel in the fridge. Blanched or cooked black salsify can be frozen.

SEASON
Organic black salsify can be harvested from early fall. It can withstand cold and can therefore be harvested until the weather makes digging impossible. It can remain in the soil throughout the winter and be harvested again when the ground has thawed.

GOES WELL WITH
Black salsify goes well with, for example, lemon, apples, mushrooms, spinach, kale, cranberries, potatoes, garlic, parsley, butter, Parmesan cheese, beef, game, and bacon.

19 ways of preparing black salsify

BOIL
Peel, then boil
Peel black salsify with a potato peeler under running water and cut into chunks. Place immediately into a large bowl of water with lemon juice to stop discoloration. Boil black salsify in a saucepan of salted water until soft. Drain. Serve with, for example, butter flavored with lemon juice, grated lemon zest, and mixed herbs or hollandaise sauce.

With butter, scallion, and parsley
Peel and chop black salsify. Boil in a saucepan of salted water or stock until soft. Drain. Add a pat of butter, thinly sliced scallion, and chopped parsley. Season with salt and pepper.

With savoy cabbage, onion, cream, mustard, and parsley
Peel and chop black salsify. Boil in a saucepan of salted water until soft. Drain well. In a skillet, fry shredded savoy cabbage, onion, and butter for a few minutes. Stir in the black salsify. Pour over cream and simmer until the cream has thickened. Season with Dijon mustard, salt, and pepper. Garnish with chopped parsley.

With white wine, stock, thyme, bay leaves, and lemon
Peel and chop black salsify. Boil in a saucepan with a splash of white wine, vegetable stock, thyme, bay leaves, and some grated lemon zest until soft. Allow the black salsify to cool in the liquid, then store in the fridge. To serve, fry the black salsify over a high heat or heat in water with a little butter. Goes well with, for example, steamed fish and spinach or poached eggs and melted butter.

With butter, hazelnuts, and scallion
Melt butter in a skillet, add coarsely chopped hazelnuts, and cook until the butter has browned. Stir in chopped cooked black salsify and sliced scallion. Goes well with, for example, fish fried in butter.

With gremolata
Combine chopped cooked black salsify with gremolata (finely chopped garlic, parsley, grated lemon zest, and olive oil). Served with, for example, air-dried ham or lamb.

With arugula, orange, vinaigrette, and pumpkin seeds
In a bowl, combine chopped cooked black salsify, shredded arugula leaves, and filleted orange segments. Whisk together 1 part red wine vinegar, 3 parts olive oil, salt, and pepper. Add the vinaigrette to the bowl and stir well to combine. Sprinkle with roasted pumpkin seeds.

In soups and stews
Slice cold cooked black salsify and stir into soups or stews.

With lemon dressing, crème fraîche, onion, and dill or chive
Cut cold cooked black salsify into strips and place in a bowl. Whisk together 1 part lemon juice, 2 parts olive oil, salt, and pepper. Stir in crème fraîche and finely chopped onion. Pour the dressing over the black salsify and sprinkle with chopped dill or chives. Goes well with, for example, fish.

With mayonnaise, dill, and lemon
In a bowl, combine chopped, cold cooked black salsify with olive oil, salt, and pepper. Flavor mayonnaise with chopped dill and squeezed lemon juice. Serve the mayonnaise with the black salsify.

FRY
With garlic, thyme, and spinach or kale
Peel black salsify and cut into thin strips. Fry in oil and butter together with crushed garlic until soft. Add thyme leaves and shredded lettuce or kale before serving.

Black salsify with butter, hazelnuts, and scallion. >

With onion, garlic, thyme, rosemary, apple juice, and honey

Peel black salsify and cut into strips. Lightly fry in butter until golden brown together with finely chopped onions, sliced garlic, thyme, and rosemary twigs. Add a large glass of apple juice. Simmer for about 15 minutes, until completely tender. Add water if it becomes too dry. Season with honey, salt, and pepper.

With onion, apple, and cranberry

Peel and chop black salsify. Boil in a saucepan of salted water until soft. Drain. Fry the black salsify in butter until golden brown along with thinly sliced onion and apple. Season with salt and pepper. Place in a bowl and stir in cranberries. Goes well with, for example, burgers.

With mushrooms, sourdough bread, onion, and garlic

Peel and chop black salsify. Boil in a saucepan of salted water until soft. Drain. Fry the mushrooms in butter until golden brown. Add black salsify, diced sourdough bread, chopped onion, and crushed garlic. Fry until the black salsify has browned. Season with salt and pepper.

With parsley

Fry cooked black salsify in butter until golden brown. Season with salt and pepper, and stir in some chopped parsley.

ROAST
With garlic

Peel and chop black salsify. Place on a baking tray and add olive oil, crushed garlic, salt and pepper. Roast at 300 °F (150 °C), or until soft, then increase the heat to 400 °F (200 °C), or until the black salsify has turned golden.

With cream and Parmesan

Place boiled black salsify on a greased baking tray or in an ovenproof dish. Cover with cream, season with salt and pepper, and sprinkle with grated Parmesan cheese. Roast at 400 °F (200 °C), for about 15 minutes, or until the cheese is crisp and golden brown.

With butter, breadcrumbs, and Parmesan

Place cooked black salsify in a greased ovenproof dish. Stir together 1 part softened butter, 1 part breadcrumbs, and 2 parts grated Parmesan cheese. Spread the mixture onto the black salsify. Roast at 400 °F (200 °C) for about 10 minutes, or until golden brown and crisp.

DEEP-FRY
Coat with flour, egg, and breadcrumbs

Turn cooked black salsify first in all-purpose flour, then in a whisked egg, and finally in breadcrumbs. Deep-fry in hot oil until golden brown. Drain on paper towels. Season with salt and pepper.

See also the asparagus tips on pages 118–119.

CELERY ROOT

This knobbly root is an often-overlooked vegetable. It can appear quite intimidating with its thick skin and muddy surface, but it is in fact one of our most versatile and nutritious roots. Celery root is harvested and sold as early as high summer, often with stems and leaves. The leaves are removed before they arrive in the stores in the fall, when celery root is fully ripe and ready for winter storage.

Celery root is very strongly flavored so it should be used in small amounts. Not everyone is fond of its dominant, nutty flavor, but most people will enjoy the vegetable served in small portions with potatoes or other root vegetables.

Raw celery root has a fantastic crunch and a super-nutty, celery flavor which makes it perfect for salads and slaws. Cooked, it takes on a slight sweetness that works well when mashed, baked, or roasted. The easiest cooking method is to boil celery root strips in a saucepan of salted water or stock until soft, then coat in butter and season with salt and pepper, or simply add to soups, stews, or stocks, or serve as a creamy purée. Celery root can also be roasted in the oven with its skin on.

Use celery root stems in the same way as celery stems. However, both the taste and texture are stronger.

STORING
Store celery root in the fridge, preferably in a damp towel. Puréed, parboiled, or cooked celery root is fine to freeze.

SEASON
Celery root is a difficult crop to grow, as it requires warm, moist soil, but a cool climate. It is generally harvested in fall or winter, and is available in stores well into late winter.

GOES WELL WITH
Celery root goes well with, for example, potatoes, mushrooms, apple, pears, ginger, mayonnaise, mustard, nuts, blue cheese, cream, egg, smoked salmon, lamb, and ham.

Celery root with thyme, Parmesan, and mayonnaise.

20 ways of preparing celery root

RAW
With apple, shallot, mayonnaise, mustard, vinegar, and walnuts
Peel and coarsely grate celery root and apple. Mix with finely chopped shallot in a bowl. Coat with mayonnaise and flavor with Dijon mustard, a splash of vinegar, salt, and pepper. Sprinkle with crushed walnuts. Goes well with ham sandwiches.

With scallion, baby leaf spinach, mustard, and vinaigrette
Peel celery root and cut into thin strips. In a bowl, combine with thinly sliced scallion and baby leaf spinach. Whisk together 1 part whole grain Dijon mustard, 1 part vinegar, 3 parts olive oil, salt, and pepper. Add to the bowl.

PICKLE
With vinegar, sugar, chili, and ginger
Peel celery root and cut into ½-inch (1.25 cm) thick slices. Boil in a saucepan of salted water. Drain. Place the celery root in a preserving jar with a lid. Boil 1 part vinegar, 2 parts powdered sugar, 3 parts water, sliced chili, and ginger in a saucepan. Cover the celery root with the hot liquid, secure the lid tightly and set aside for at least one day. Goes well with salads, stirred into mayonnaise, or with game instead of cranberries. Can be stored in the fridge for up to three months.

BOIL
With butter, thyme, and parsley
Peel celery root and cut into cubes. Boil in a saucepan of salted water until soft. Pour off most of the water. Add a pat of butter, a few sprigs of thyme, and chopped parsley. Season with salt and pepper.

With stock, apple juice, and cream
Peel and chop celery root. Boil in a saucepan with vegetable stock, a little apple juice, and cream until soft. Drain and save the liquid. Mash to the desired purée consistency, adding some of the liquid as required. Season with salt and pepper. Goes well with fried mushrooms.

With potato, mushrooms, red onion, mustard, and vinaigrette
Peel and cut into chunks an equal quantity of celery root and potatoes. Boil in a saucepan of salted water until soft. Drain. In a bowl, mix with thinly sliced raw mushrooms and sliced red onion. Whisk together 1 part Dijon mustard, 1 part vinegar, 3 parts olive oil, salt, and pepper. Add the vinaigrette to the bowl.

With potato, cream, and butter
Peel and chop celery root and potatoes. Boil in separate saucepans in salted water until soft. Mash the potatoes and the celery root and stir together. Stir in warm cream and butter. Season with salt and pepper.

With cream, Parmesan, and bacon
Peel celery root and cut into thin strips. Boil quickly in a saucepan of salted water. Drain. Heat cream in a saucepan. Stir in the celery root and grated Parmesan cheese. Season with salt and pepper, and top with crispy fried diced smoked bacon.

With milk
Peel and slice celery root. Place in a saucepan, cover with milk, and cook until soft. Drain the milk and save. Mash the celery root until smooth, adding a little of the milk to make a firm purée. Season with salt and pepper. Goes well with baked mushrooms.

FRY
With potato and apple
Peel and coarsely grate an equal amount of celery root and potatoes plus a little apple. Squeeze out the liquid and put into a bowl. Season with salt and pepper. Heat butter and oil in a skillet. Shape the mixture into a thin pancake and fry over a medium heat, for about five minutes. Turn over the pancake and fry on the other side until golden brown.

With onion, apple, vinaigrette, walnuts, and parsley

Peel and thinly slice celery root. Fry in oil together with finely chopped onion until soft. Add thin apple slices and sauté until warm and soft. Transfer to a bowl. Whisk together 1 part red wine vinegar, 3 parts olive oil, salt, and pepper. Add the vinaigrette and sprinkle with chopped walnuts and parsley.

With mushrooms, garlic, and parsley

Peel celery root and cut into ½-inch (1.25 cm) thick slices. Fry in butter with chopped mushrooms and crushed garlic until golden brown and soft. Season with salt and pepper, and sprinkle with chopped parsley.

With savoy cabbage, garlic, and thyme

Peel celery root and cut into ½-inch (1.25 cm) thick slices. Fry in olive oil along with coarsely shredded savoy cabbage, finely chopped garlic, and thyme until golden brown. Season with salt and pepper. Add a few tablespoons of water, cover, and simmer gently until done.

With flour, egg, and breadcrumbs

Peel celery root and cut into ¼ inch (6 mm) thick slices. Boil the slices in a saucepan of salted water until soft. Cool in iced water and dry with paper towels. Coat the celery root slices first in all-purpose flour, then in whisked egg, and finally in breadcrumbs. Fry in oil until golden brown. Season with salt and pepper.

ROAST
With butter and hazelnuts

Thoroughly scrub unpeeled celery root and place on a baking tray. Roast at 300 °F (150 °C) until soft. Brown butter in a skillet, add chopped hazelnuts and fry. Halve the roasted celery root and cover with the hazelnut butter. Season with salt and pepper.

With thyme, Parmesan, and mayonnaise

Peel celery root and cut into wedges. Place on a baking tray or in an ovenproof dish with olive oil, thyme, salt, and pepper. Roast at 300 °F (150 °C) for 20–30 minutes, or until soft and golden brown. Add grated Parmesan cheese. Serve with mayonnaise.

With garlic, butter, and olive oil

Peel and chop celery root. Place on pieces of aluminum foil with crushed garlic, butter, and olive oil. Season with salt. Fold into parcels. Bake at 400 °F (200 °C) for 20–30 minutes.

With potato, onion, mushrooms, garlic, cream, and milk

Peel and thinly slice celery root, potatoes, and onions. Fry mushrooms in butter until golden brown. Put into an ovenproof dish together with crushed garlic, salt, and pepper. Cover with a mixture equal parts cream and milk. Bake at 350 °F (175 °C) for 30–40 minutes, or until the vegetables are soft and golden brown.

BROIL
Whole with flavored butter

Broil small, whole, scrubbed, and unpeeled celery root directly under the broiler or wrapped in aluminum foil until soft. Halve and serve with flavored butter (see page 179).

DEEP-FRY
As chips

Peel and very thinly slice celery root. Rinse in cold water, drain, and dry. Once completely dry, deep-fry in hot oil until golden brown. Drain on paper towels. Goes well with crème fraîche and extra cream.

ARTICHOKE

Artichokes, also known as French or green artichokes, are beautifully colored, olive green vegetables with a mild, slightly nutty flavor and a delicate sweetness and acidity that really does make the mouth water. They are the inflorescences of a variety of thistle, harvested just before they blossom. Their leaves, or bracts, have a lower fleshy end that is edible. They form around the base or "heart," while the fuzzy, inedible "choke" on top of the heart is not edible. Artichokes are nutritional "powerhouses," and at their best from summer to fall. Choose artichokes that feel firm and heavy, with tightly packed leaves. Don't be put off by any red or black coloring, but brown coloring is a sign that the artichoke is spoiling.

To prepare the artichoke, snip off the tips of the leaves and remove the small leaves at the stem—the artichoke should be able to sit flush on the work surface. Cut away any excess stem.

Artichokes are very easy to eat. Once cooked, simply pull the leaves from the plant, dip in your favorite vinaigrette and gently pull and scrape out the creamy artichoke flesh with your teeth. Now cut into the delicious heart—the caviar of the artichoke. Be sure to serve with lots of melted butter.

STORING
Artichokes are sensitive to dry conditions. They should be stored only for a short time in a chilled and humid environment. Splash with water and store wrapped in a kitchen towel in the fridge.

SEASON
Artichokes are grown as perennials and the season depends on climate and variety. Warm coastal areas allow harvesting in late spring.

GOES WELL WITH
Artichokes go well with tomatoes, fennel, lemon, herbs, capers, vinaigrette, mayonnaise, olive oil, butter, goat cheese, prosciutto, fish, seafood, and anchovies.

< Artichoke with vinegar, shallot, and basil.

21 ways of preparing artichoke

LARGE ARTICHOKES

Boil whole

Break off the artichoke stalk as close to the bottom as possible. Remove the tough outer leaves and cut away a bit of the top. Boil in water, with a dash of lemon juice and salt (use 1 teaspoon of salt per 2 pints/1 liter of water) for about 30–40 minutes, or until the leaves come away easily when pulled and the heart is tender when tested with a skewer. Alternatively, cook in vegetable stock or equal parts water and white wine. Let cool a little before eating. Remove the choke before serving.

With butter and lemon

In a bowl, combine softened butter with lemon juice, grated lemon zest, salt, and pepper. Dip artichoke leaves into the butter.

With butter, anchovies, and lemon

In a bowl, combine softened butter with chopped anchovies, lemon juice, salt, and pepper. Dip artichoke leaves into the butter.

With butter and tapenade

In a bowl, combine softened butter with tapenade, salt, and pepper. Dip artichoke leaves into the butter.

With butter and Parmesan

In a bowl, combine softened butter with grated Parmesan cheese, salt, and pepper. Dip artichoke leaves into the butter.

With butter, herbs, and garlic

In a bowl, combine softened butter with chopped herbs, garlic, salt, and pepper. Dip artichoke leaves into the butter.

With vinegar, shallot, and basil

In a bowl, whisk together 1 part red wine vinegar, 3 parts olive oil, salt, and pepper in a bowl. Stir in finely chopped shallot and shredded basil. Dip artichoke leaves into the vinaigrette.

With pesto

Dip artichoke leaves in pesto.

BABY ARTICHOKES

Cook whole

Remove the tough outer leaves and cut a bit off the top of the artichoke. Peel the stem with a potato peeler. Cook in a saucepan of salted water for about 20 minutes, or until soft. The leaves should come away easily when pulled. Lift out the artichokes and let cool. Remove the choke and inner leaves before serving.

With garlic, chili, lemon, and parsley

Remove the tough outer leaves and cut a bit off the top of the artichokee. Peel the stem with a potato peeler. Cut the artichokes in half and scrape out the choke from the center. Sauté chopped garlic and chili in olive oil. Add the artichoke halves and cook for a few minutes more. Add water, lemon juice, and salt. Cover and simmer for about 20 minutes, or until soft. Top with chopped parsley.

With garlic, yellow onion, white wine, tomato, and basil

Remove the tough outer leaves and cut a bit off the top of the artichoke. Peel the stem with a potato peeler. Cut the artichokes in half and scrape out the choke from the center. Sauté chopped garlic and yellow onion in olive oil. Add the artichoke halves and cook for a few minutes more. Add a dash of white wine and chopped tomatoes. Cover and simmer for about 20 minutes, or until soft. Top with chopped basil.

Fry with garlic

Remove the tough outer leaves and cut a bit off the top of the artichoke. Peel the stem with a potato peeler. Cut the artichokes in half and scrape out the choke from the center, then slice the artichokes. Sauté in olive oil and garlic until soft and golden brown. Season with salt and pepper. Goes well with fish or bread.

ARTICHOKE HEARTS

Boil
Break off the stems as close to the base of the artichoke as possible. Remove the tough outer leaves and cut off the leaves above the heart. Remove the artichoke base leaves with a small sharp knife. Rub with lemon to prevent discoloration. Cook in equal parts of salted water and white wine, with a dash of olive oil, until soft.

Purée
Cook and chop artichoke hearts, then pulse with olive oil in a food processor or a blender. Season with salt and pepper. Goes well with fish or bread.

With tomato, red onion, basil, Parmesan, and vinaigrette
Cook and dice artichoke hearts, then combine with halved cherry tomatoes, thinly sliced red onion, basil, and grated Parmesan cheese in a bowl. Whisk together 1 part balsamic vinegar, 2 parts olive oil, salt, and pepper. Stir the vinaigrette into the vegetables. Goes well with cold cuts.

With prosciutto, lettuce, scallion, vinaigrette, and goat cheese
Fry prosciutto slices in a skillet in olive oil until crispy. Drain on paper towels. In a bowl, combine cubed, cooked artichoke hearts with lettuce leaves and sliced scallion. Whisk together 1 part vinegar, 3 parts olive oil, salt, and pepper. Toss the salad in the vinaigrette. Top with crumbled goat cheese and crispy prosciutto.

With red onion and tomato
Thread cubed artichoke hearts onto a skewer with red onion wedges and cherry tomatoes. Coat in olive oil, and season with salt and pepper. Broil and serve with meat or fish.

With tomato, red onion, herbs, vinaigrette, bread, and egg
In a bowl, combine cooked, sliced artichoke hearts, sliced tomato, sliced red onion, and chopped herbs. Whisk together 1 part vinegar, 3 parts olive oil, salt, and pepper. Toss the salad in the vinaigrette. Serve on a slice of bread with a poached or soft-boiled egg.

With shrimps, shallot, dill, mayonnaise, and potato chips
Coat a whole cooked artichoke heart in olive oil and put on a plate. Season with salt and pepper. In a bowl combine shrimp, finely chopped shallot, and chopped dill. Place a dollop of mayonnaise in the center of the artichoke heart, and spoon over the shrimp salad. Top with crushed potato chips.

With garlic and tomato salad
Sauté cooked artichoke heart chunks in olive oil. Season with salt, pepper, and chopped garlic. Place on a plate, and top with tomato salad.

With Parmesan, garlic, basil, and olive oil
Combine cooked hearts with grated Parmesan cheese, chopped garlic, basil, and a dash of olive oil. Delicious on a slice of bread.

FAVA BEANS

Kidney-shaped fava beans, also known as broad beans, sit inside a thick leathery pod. They need to be "double podded" before preparing. To do so, cook the beans for a few minutes in lightly salted water, crain, then chill in iced water before draining again. Slit each pod along its seam and run your thumb inside the pod to push the beans out. For the second stage, you need to remove the thin skin that covers each individual bean. If the fava beans are not quite ripe, or have been harvested too early, shelling may be time-consuming, but the fava beans' delicious flavor, pure green color, and tender consistency are worth the effort.

Fava beans are a great decorative addition to a salad, omelet, soup, or pasta. Prepare them just before serving to keep them firm. Cooked fava beans seasoned with a dash of olive oil, dill, salt, and pepper are a tasty topping for a slice of sourdough bread.

Fresh fava beans can be placed straight into the freezer. Thaw the frozen beans before podding and hulling.

When choosing fava beans, don't worry about any black marks you see on the outside of the pod. Look instead for crisp and firm pods.

STORING
Store fava beans wrapped in a kitchen towel in the fridge. Blanched and raw fava beans can be frozen.

SEASON
Fava beans are grown over the summer months.

GOES WELL WITH
Fava beans go well with fennel, leek, tomatoes, lemon, herbs, goat cheese, feta cheese, hollandaise sauce, butter, and olive oil.

Fava beans with tomato, garlic, basil, pasta, and goat cheese. >

12 ways of preparing fava beans

BOIL

Boil and pod

Hull and remove the beans from the thick pods. Cook in a saucepan of salted water for 2–4 minutes. Chill in iced water and skin by popping them out of their skins.

With yellow onion, garlic, white wine, tomato, butter, and basil

Sauté chopped onion and sliced garlic in olive oil over a medium heat until soft, but not browned. Pod, skin, and cook fava beans, and add with a generous amount of white wine. Cook gently and add cubed tomatoes with a pat of butter. Simmer until the tomatoes are tender. Season with salt and pepper, and top with torn basil leaves.

With bacon, red onion, vinegar, pasta, and Parmesan

Pod, skin, and cook fava beans. In a bowl, combine the beans with cooked smoked bacon cubes and finely chopped red onion. Season with salt, pepper, and a few drops of vinegar. Stir in freshly cooked pasta. Sprinkle with grated Parmesan cheese.

With egg, red onion, parsley, and butter

Pod, skin, and cook fava beans. In a bowl, combine the beans with chopped hard-boiled eggs, finely chopped red onion, and chopped parsley. Season with salt and pepper, and drizzle with melted butter. Goes well with fish.

With tomato, garlic, basil, pasta, and goat cheese

Pod, skin, and cook fava beans. In a bowl, combine the beans with halved cherry tomatoes, finely chopped garlic, chopped basil leaves, a generous amount of olive oil, salt, and pepper. Stir into freshly cooked pasta, and top with crumbled goat cheese.

With olive oil and dill

Pod, skin, and cook fava beans. Place in a blender with olive oil and blend to a smooth purée. Add chopped dill, season with salt and pepper, and pulse again. Goes well with bread.

With fennel, cherry tomato, and basil

Pod, skin, and cook fava beans. Sauté over a medium heat with thinly sliced fennel, halved cherry tomatoes, shredded basil, and olive oil. Season with salt and pepper.

With cucumber, scallion, shrimps, dill, and lemon

Pod, skin, and cook fava beans. In a bowl, combine the beans with seeded and cubed cucumber, sliced scallion, shrimp, and finely chopped dill. Dress with olive oil, lemon juice, salt, and pepper.

FRY

With red onion and garlic

Pod, skin, and cook fava beans. Sauté in olive oil with chopped red onion and garlic until they begin to brown. Season with salt and pepper. Goes well with pasta.

With anchovies, garlic, and parsley

Sauté chopped anchovies, garlic, and parsley in butter for a few minutes. Add peeled and cooked fava beans and cook for a few minutes. Season with pepper.

With garlic and romaine lettuce

Pod, skin, and cook fava beans. Sauté in olive oil and a pat of butter with sliced garlic. Chop romaine lettuce and toss with the beans. Serve with fish or chicken.

BAKE

With goat cheese

Pod, skin, and cook fava beans. and place in an ovenproof dish. Drizzle with olive oil and scatter with crumbled goat cheese. Bake until the cheese starts to melt. Spread the mixture onto sourdough bread.

BROCCOLI

Broccoli is a vegetable of two halves: the delicate florets and the woody stem.

The coarse and woody end of a broccoli stem is the only part you should remove. The rest of the head is edible. You can peel the stem easily with a sharp knife or a potato peeler, and will be left with a mild and bright green delicacy, perfectly edible raw. But, as with broccoli in general, the color and flavor will benefit from cooking gently in salted water. Lengthy cooking will reduce the flavor, texture, and nutritional value.

The stem is delicious in a salad with vinaigrette, on its own with a pat of butter, or with olive oil and a pinch of salt. It can also be included with the rest of the broccoli head in a vegetable soup.

Broccoli florets can be fried raw, without being boiled first. Just cut them into slightly smaller florets so they can soften without browning too quickly.

STORING
Store broccoli in the fridge, preferably wrapped in a kitchen towel; the vegetable is sensitive to the ethylene gas produced by most fruits, potatoes, and onions. The gas will hasten the deterioration process. You can blanch and freeze broccoli.

SEASON
Broccoli is grown from late summer into fall and will withstand light frost. It is grown year-round as a greenhouse plant.

GOES WELL WITH
Broccoli goes well with bell pepper, onion, garlic, lemon, chili, ginger, capers, light soy sauce, sesame, nuts, blue cheese, Parmesan cheese, egg, bacon, and anchovies.

23 ways of preparing broccoli

RAW
With olive oil and lemon
Thinly slice broccoli and coat with olive oil, grated lemon zest, salt, and black pepper. Rub the oil into the broccoli.

BOIL
Stems with olive oil
Remove the coarse and woody part of the broccoli stem. Peel and chop the remaining stem with a sharp knife and cook in lightly salted water until soft. Transfer to a plate, drizzle with olive oil and season with salt.

With egg and butter
Cut off the coarsest part of the broccoli stem and peel the rest with a sharp knife or a potato peeler. Cut the broccoli into florets with long stems and cook in salted water until tender. Arrange on a plate with halved hard-boiled eggs. Drizzle with melted butter. Season with salt and pepper.

With lemon dressing, hot sauce, and cashews
In a bowl, whisk together 1 part lemon juice, 2 parts olive oil, and a few drops of hot sauce. Toss cooked broccoli in the dressing and add chopped cashew nuts.

With fish sauce and olive oil
Season cooked broccoli with a few drops of fish sauce, olive oil, and sea salt.

With sweet chili and soy
In a bowl, whisk equal parts sweet chili and light soy sauce. Stir in the cooked broccoli.

With mayonnaise, lemon or mustard
In a bowl, whisk together mayonnaise, grated lemon zest, and a dash of fresh lemon juice or Dijon mustard. Season with salt and pepper. Serve with cooked broccoli.

With blue cheese, vinegar, olive oil, and walnuts
Blend blue cheese with a few drops of water. Season with vinegar, olive oil, and pepper. Turn the broccoli florets in the sauce and top with crushed walnuts.

With deep-fried garlic
Scatter deep-fried garlic (see page 132) over cooked broccoli. Season with olive oil and salt.

With sesame seeds, mayonnaise, and soy
Fry sesame seeds in a hot skillet with a little oil. Season with salt. Combine mayonnaise, light soy sauce, and sesame oil. Stir in the sesame seeds. Serve as a dip.

With leek, stock, lemon, and cream or olive oil
Chop broccoli into florets and thinly slice the stems. Sauté in olive oil for a few minutes with sliced leek. Cover with stock and simmer for 15 minutes, or until soft. Purée the soup, adding more water if necessary, and flavor with lemon juice, salt, and pepper, and perhaps a dash of cream or olive oil.

With coconut milk, red curry paste, stock, carrot, and yellow onion
Heat coconut milk in a saucepan. Add red curry paste and a stock cube. Cook broccoli florets, sliced carrot, and chopped onion in the mixture until soft. Delicious as a soup, or serve with rice.

With cherry tomato, onion, and vinaigrette
Coarsely grate broccoli and place in a bowl. Heat salted water in a saucepan and pour it over the broccoli. Let steep for a few minutes. Drain the broccoli and combine in a bowl with halved cherry tomatoes and finely chopped onion. Whisk together 1 part vinegar, 3 parts olive oil, salt, and pepper. Toss the vegetables in the vinaigrette to combine well.

< Broccoli with chili, cashews, garlic, and soy.

With celery, yellow onion, garlic, thyme, vegetable stock, and cream

Sauté broccoli florets in butter with sliced celery, yellow onion, chopped garlic, and thyme. Cover with vegetable stock and simmer for 10 minutes, or until the broccoli is soft. Blend the soup in a blender until smooth, adding more stock or cream to reach the desired consistency. Season with salt and pepper.

With yellow onion, garlic, ginger, white wine, vegetable stock, and potato

Sauté sliced yellow onion, and finely chopped garlic and ginger in olive oil until soft. Add a dash of white wine and cook for a few minutes. Pour in vegetable stock and cook for another 10 minutes. Add broccoli and cold, cooked potato and cook until soft. Season with salt and pepper.

FRY
With bacon

Peel and slice broccoli stems, then sauté with chopped bacon in olive oil until the broccoli is soft. Season with pepper.

With garlic and almonds

Sauté broccoli florets and thinly sliced stems in olive oil until soft. Add sliced garlic and sauté for a few minutes more. Garnish with flaked almonds and toss. Season with salt and pepper.

With bacon, egg, and Parmesan

Fry bacon until crispy, then remove from the skillet. Thinly slice the broccoli and fry in the bacon fat until soft. In a bowl, whisk together eggs, a little water, salt, and pepper. Pour over the broccoli and, using a turner, pull from the edges into the center. Repeat several times. Reduce the heat and continue cooking until the eggs are set. Scatter over the bacon and grated Parmesan cheese.

With chili, cashews, garlic, and soy

Cut off the toughest part of the broccoli stem and peel the rest with a sharp knife or potato peeler. Cut the broccoli into florets with long stalks. Boil in salted water until soft. Drain well. Fry the broccoli with shredded fresh chili in oil for a minute. Stir in roasted cashew nuts and sprinkle with deep-fried garlic (see page 132). Season with a dash of light soy sauce.

With coconut and chili

Gently fry broccoli florets in coconut oil until soft. Add roasted coconut flakes, chopped red chili, salt, and pepper.

ROAST
With dill and lemon

Toss broccoli florets with olive oil, salt, and pepper and transfer to a baking tray. Roast at 400 °F (200 °C) for about 12 minutes, or until soft and golden brown. Peel the stems and slice thinly. Plunge into iced water, then drain. In a bowl, combine the florets and sliced stems with chopped dill and lemon juice.

With crème fraîche, ginger und cilantro

Toss broccoli florets and thinly sliced stems with olive oil, season with salt and pepper, and transfer to a baking tray. Roast at 400 °F (200 °C) for 10–15 minutes, or until crisp. Season the crème fraîche with grated ginger, chopped cilantro, salt and pepper. Serve with the broccoli.

See also cauliflower tips on pages 113–115.

CAULIFLOWER

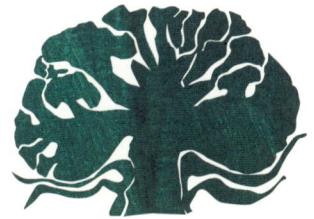

From baked whole in the oven, to pickled and preserved in vinegar, cauliflower is one of our most versatile vegetables, and its florets, stem, and even the protective leaves are all edible. It can be boiled, sautéed, broiled, or deep-fried. But it doesn't actually need to be cooked: raw florets are delicious in salads, or as part of a crudité platter served with dips which maximize the taste and texture. Retain the flavor when cooking cauliflower by avoiding lengthy boiling, which releases an unpleasant aroma and increases the vegetable's cabbage flavor. The taste of cauliflower changes depending on how it is cooked. Quickly steamed, pan-fried, broiled, or deep-fried cauliflower florets have a mild flavor, which can be encouraged by soaking the stems and florets in iced water before cooking. Iced water can also be used to perk up a cauliflower that is past its best.

The mild stem can be peeled, sliced, and enjoyed in soups and stews.

Romanesco broccoli, which is also known as **Roman cauliflower**, has a light green, spiral-shaped head that looks a bit like a miniature Christmas tree. It is milder in flavor than either cauliflower or broccoli. Boil or steam quickly to preserve its flavor and color.

STORING
Store cauliflower in the fridge, preferably in a kitchen towel. Keep the protective outer leaves on. Cauliflower can be blanched and frozen.

SEASON
Cauliflower will only grow in consistently temperate temperatures that are neither too hot, nor too cold. It is generally grown as a fall crop.

GOES WELL WITH
Cauliflower goes well with spinach, tomatoes, potatoes, herbs, curry, cumin, saffron, chili, raisins, almonds, couscous, capers, anchovies, fish, shrimp, and fish roe.

32 ways of preparing cauliflower

RAW

With shallot, pomegranate, baby leaf spinach, and vinaigrette

Coarsely chop cauliflower. In a bowl, combine with chopped shallot, pomegranate seeds, and baby leaf spinach. Whisk together 1 part white wine vinegar, 3 parts olive oil, salt, and pepper. Stir into the bowl.

With red onion, tomato, arugula, olive oil, and lemon juice

Thinly slice cauliflower. In a bowl, combine it with halved cherry tomatoes, arugula, and olive oil. Season with salt, pepper, and lemon juice.

With carrot, dill or chive, mayonnaise, crème fraîche, mustard, and vinegar

Thinly slice cauliflower. In a bowl, combine it with coarsely grated carrot and chopped dill or chives. Stir together equal parts mayonnaise and crème fraîche. Season with Dijon mustard, a couple of drops of vinegar, salt, and pepper. Add to the bowl. Goes well with broiled fish.

In potato salad

Thinly sliced raw cauliflower will make the potato salad taste fresher.

With apple, onion, lentils, and lemon

Thinly slice cauliflower. In a bowl, combine it with apples, onion, and cooked lentils. Season with salt and pepper. Whisk together 1 part lemon juice, 2 parts olive oil, salt, and pepper. Stir the sauce into the bowl.

With red onion, Chinese cabbage, kimchi base, soy, vinegar, and ginger

Thinly slice cauliflower. In a bowl, combine it with sliced red onion and shredded Chinese cabbage. Whisk together equal parts kimchi base, light soy sauce, white wine vinegar, oil, and a pinch of grated ginger. Toss the salad with the vinaigrette. Goes well with fried fish.

< Cauliflower with butter, gherkin, and dill; whole roasted cauliflower.

With chive, cress, and lemon dressing

Coarsely chop cauliflower. In a bowl, combine it with finely chopped chives, and garden cress. Whisk together 2 parts lemon juice, 2 parts olive oil, salt, and pepper. Toss the cauliflower mixture with the dressing. Goes well with shrimp salad or fried fish.

With horseradish, dill, and lemon dressing

Chop cauliflower. In a bowl, combine it with freshly grated horseradish and dill. Whisk together 2 parts lemon juice, 2 parts olive oil, salt, and pepper. Toss the cauliflower mixture with the dressing. Goes well with fish.

With mustard or dill, and boiled potato

Mix thinly sliced raw cauliflower with the mustard or dill, and boiled potato. Goes well with salmon.

With mustard or dill sauce and potato

Mix thinly sliced raw cauliflower with a mustard or dill sauce, and boiled potato. Goes well with fish.

With radish, ricotta, herbs, and croutons

Thinly slice cauliflower and radishes, then soak in iced water for a couple of minutes. Blend ricotta cheese with herbs of your choice. Spread ricotta mix on a plate and top with cauliflower and radish slices. Season with salt and pepper and drizzle with olive oil. Top with herbs and croutons. Goes well with broiled vegetables.

PICKLE

With vinegar, sugar, dill seeds, leek, peppercorns, and spinach or arugula

Thinly slice cauliflower, place in a preserving jar with a lid. Combine 1 part vinegar, 2 parts powdered sugar, and 3 parts water in a saucepan and bring to the boil with dill seeds and black peppercorns. Pour the hot mixture over the cauliflower and let stand for at least a couple of hours. Drain and combine cauliflower with thinly sliced leek and chopped spinach or arugula. Season with salt and pepper. Will keep in the fridge for up to one month.

BOIL

With garlic, lemon, and herbs
Coarsely chop cauliflower and cook in a saucepan of salted water for about 15 seconds. Drain and add a pat of butter. Add chopped garlic and lemon zest. Combine thoroughly and season with salt, pepper, and herbs of your choice.

With butter and almonds
Chop cauliflower and cook in a saucepan of lightly salted water until soft. Drain and transfer to a plate. Add butter, coarsely chopped almonds, salt, and pepper to the saucepan and heat through. Pour over the cauliflower.

With butter, gherkin, and dill
Chop cauliflower and cook in a saucepan of lightly salted water until soft. Drain and add a pat of butter. Combine with chopped gherkins and dill. Goes well with fish.

With leek, arugula, egg, and vinaigrette
Chop cauliflower and cook in a saucepan of lightly salted water until soft. Drain. In a bowl combine with thinly sliced leek, arugula, and diced hard-boiled egg. Toss with your favorite vinaigrette. Goes well with fish.

With soy, sweet chili, and lemon
Chop cauliflower and cook in a saucepan of lightly salted water until soft. Drain. In a bowl, mix with equal parts soy and sweet chili sauces. Season with lemon juice. Goes well with baked salmon.

With potato, leek, capers, crème fraîche, mayonnaise, and lemon
Chop cauliflower and cook in a saucepan of lightly salted water until soft. Drain and cool in iced water. Combine with chopped cooked potato, sliced leek, and capers. Combine equal parts of crème fraîche and mayonnaise. Season with lemon zest, lemon juice, salt, and pepper. Toss cauliflower and potato with the dressing. Garnish with chopped dill or parsley.

With potato, butter, olive oil, dill, and lemon
Chop and cook cauliflower and potato in separate saucepans of salted water until soft. Drain and transfer both to a large bowl. Add butter and olive oil, and mash. Whisk together chopped dill, lemon zest, lemon juice, salt, and pepper, add to the bowl, and stir to combine. Goes well with fried fish.

With milk and butter
Chop and cook cauliflower in a saucepan with milk. Drain and reserve the milk. Mash the cauliflower, adding milk, until you have a smooth purée. Season with butter, salt, and pepper. Goes well with fried fish.

With yellow onion, milk, stock, butter, and lemon
Chop cauliflower and combine with sliced onion in a saucepan. Cover with milk, add a small piece of stock cube, and simmer gently. Drain and reserve the liquid. Purée the cauliflower and onion in a blender, adding some of the reserved liquid, until you have a smooth soup. Season the soup with butter, salt, pepper, and lemon juice. Serve hot or cold with chopped chives and croutons.

With kale, cream, and lemon
Thinly slice cauliflower and put into a saucepan with blanched kale leaves and a dash of cream. Simmer for 5 minutes. Season with salt, pepper, and lemon zest.

FRY

With chorizo
Chop cauliflower and sauté in olive oil with sliced chorizo.

With chili, garlic, ginger, and lemon
Coarsely chop cauliflower and sauté in olive oil or butter until it begins to brown. Stir in with finely chopped chilis, crushed garlic, grated ginger, grated lemon zest, salt, and pepper. Goes well with chicken.

With pork and baby leaf spinach

Fry chopped pork until crispy. Remove the pork and let it drain on paper towels. Add cauliflower florets and fry in the pork fat. Add shredded baby leaf spinach, return the fried pork to the pan and warm through. Season with pepper.

With curry, onion, and cilantro or parsley

Chop cauliflower and sauté in olive oil until soft. Add a large pat of butter and a generous amount of curry powder. Sauté for a couple more minutes. Stir in chopped onion and cilantro or parsley. Season with salt and pepper.

ROAST
Whole or halved

Place a whole cauliflower head or two halves with their cut sides down on a baking tray. Rub with olive oil, and season with salt and pepper. Roast at 300°F (150°C) for about 45 minutes, or until soft and golden brown. Serve with melted flavored butter (see page 179), chopped hard-boiled egg, capers, lemon dressing, and herbs or grated hard cheese.

With leek, béchamel sauce, and cheese

Chop cauliflower and cook with thinly sliced leek in a saucepan of salted water until soft. Drain and transfer to a greased ovenproof dish. Cover with a thin layer of béchamel sauce and grated hard cheese, then bake at 430°F (220°C) for about 15 minutes. Goes well with bacon and/or a green salad.

With yellow onion, fish, tomato, cream, and dill

Thinly slice cauliflower and yellow onion, then layer them on the base of a greased ovenproof dish. Top with fish fillets and sliced tomatoes. Season with salt and pepper and pour over some cream. Bake at 400°F (200°C) for about 20 minutes, or until the fish is cooked. Sprinkle with chopped dill.

With potato and garam masala

Chop cauliflower and potatoes into equal-sized cubes and place on a baking tray with olive oil. Season with garam masala, salt, and pepper. Bake at 400°F (200°C) for about 20 minutes, or until soft.

With mayonnaise, Parmesan, romaine lettuce, and croutons

Halve a cauliflower and cut it into four wedges. Coat in olive oil and place on a baking tray. Season with salt and pepper. Roast at 400°F (200°C) for about 20 minutes, or until soft. Stir grated Parmesan cheese into mayonnaise. Serve the cauliflower with the mayonnaise, shredded romaine lettuce and croutons.

DEEP-FRY
With tempura batter and flavored mayonnaise

Dip cauliflower florets in tempura batter and deep-fry until golden brown. Drain on paper towels. Serve with mayonnaise flavored with light soy sauce, sriracha, or roasted sesame seeds.

See also broccoli tips on pages 109–110.

ASPARAGUS

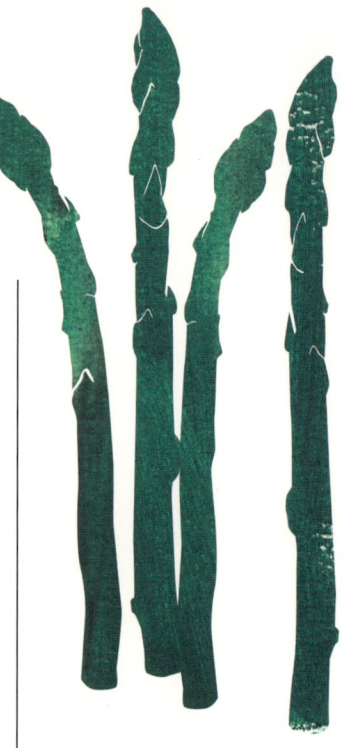

Tender asparagus is a springtime favorite and tender stems of white and green asparagus are usually found at farmers' markets in late spring. Green and white asparagus are essentially the same plant. The only difference is that white asparagus is grown underground and never exposed to light—which turns the crop green. Green asparagus, on the other hand, is grown above ground. White asparagus grows at a slower rate and develops a thicker, stronger skin than green asparagus, so it always needs to be peeled. The skins also produce a slightly bitter substance that can permeate the stems. When peeled, white asparagus is mild, while the abundant light exposure gives green asparagus its strong, grassy flavor.

Both white and green asparagus can be eaten raw. Cut off the woody parts of the stems. Peel the asparagus and cut it into very thin strips lengthwise, preferably with a mandolin slicer. Be careful when peeling and avoid leaving threads hanging loose that might be annoying when eating. Save the peel from green asparagus and use it as a base for soup. Asparagus can be cooked in a special steamer which allows the stems to stand upright, so that the thick base cooks in the water while the delicate tips are steamed. A tall, thin saucepan can also be used when cooking stems of different diameters; place the thicker ones in the water a few minutes before thinner ones.

Asparagus can be served tender or still with some "bite"—white asparagus generally needs to be cooked longer than the green.

STORING
Store asparagus in the fridge, preferably wrapped in a damp towel. To freeze, cook asparagus for 2–4 minutes in salted water, let cool, and drain. You don't need to thaw asparagus before cooking it.

SEASON
Asparagus crowns are planted several weeks before the last frost. Harvesting time is from late winter to mid spring.

GOES WELL WITH
Both green and white asparagus go well with, for example, lemon, garlic, vinegar, oil, Parmesan cheese, butter, egg, cold cuts, seafood, and smoked salmon. White asparagus goes particularly well with fish, and green asparagus with meat.

Asparagus with garlic, Parmesan, and basil. >

18 ways of preparing asparagus

RAW
Thinly sliced
Peel, cut, and thinly slice white or green asparagus stems lengthwise, preferably with a mandolin slicer. Serve with salad or fish.

BOIL
Prepare and cook green asparagus
Cut off the woody lower parts of asparagus stems where they break when the stem is flexed. Peel asparagus with a potato peeler, starting just below the tip, being careful not to leave any loose "threads." Cook in a saucepan of salted water for 2–5 minutes. The asparagus should be tender but retain some "bite."

Prepare and cook white asparagus
Cut off the woody lower parts of asparagus stems where they break when the stem is flexed. Peel asparagus with a potato peeler, starting just below the tip, being careful not to leave any loose "threads." Cook in a saucepan of salted water for 10–20 minutes depending on thickness. Asparagus should be tender but retain "bite."

With yellow onion, white wine, stock, and cream
Peel green asparagus with a potato peeler, starting just below the tip. Save the peel. Chop the asparagus. Sauté in a saucepan in olive oil together with chopped yellow onion. Add a dash of white wine and cover with vegetable stock. Simmer for 10 minutes. Add a splash of cream together with the peel and simmer for about 5 minutes, or until the asparagus is soft. Stir and strain. Season with salt and pepper.

In risotto
Slice and cook green or white asparagus as described above, then stir into a risotto.

In oil
Heat oil in a saucepan. Add white or green asparagus peel. Turn off the heat and let stand for 30 minutes. When cold, place the oil in a jar and marinate for 2–3 days. Strain. Use asparagus oil in salad dressings, homemade mayonnaise, or drizzle over cooked fish.

FRY
With garlic, Parmesan, and lemon
Halve stems of peeled white or green asparagus lengthwise. Fry in olive oil with crushed garlic until soft and golden brown. Season with salt and pepper. Scatter with grated Parmesan cheese and squeeze over lemon juice.

With egg and cheese
Cook and chop asparagus, then fry over a high heat in a skillet with butter. Whisk together eggs, a dash of water, salt, and pepper. Pour the mixture over the asparagus and, with a turner, pull the egg from the edges toward the center. Repeat several times. Lower the heat and fry until the eggs have set. Sprinkle the omelet with grated cheese.

With prosciutto
Wrap prosciutto around cooked white or green asparagus. Fry in a skillet with a little olive oil for a few minutes.

ROAST
With garlic, Parmesan, and basil
Put stems of peeled white or green asparagus, olive oil, crushed garlic, salt, and pepper into an ovenproof dish. Roast at 350 °F (175 °C) until soft and golden brown. Add grated Parmesan cheese and top with shredded basil.

BROIL
Prepare for broiling
Both green and white asparagus are very tasty broiled. Prepare white asparagus by peeling thoroughly and cooking quickly in salted water, then halving lengthwise before broiling.

Peel green asparagus only if its skin is thick and tough. Coat the asparagus stems with oil and place them under the broiler. Arrange on a platter and season with flavorings of your choice, for example, olive oil, lemon juice, fresh herbs, salt, and pepper.

GOES WELL WITH WARM ASPARAGUS

With vinaigrette and Parmesan
Whisk together 1 part balsamic vinegar, 3 parts olive oil, salt, and pepper. Pour the vinaigrette over the asparagus. Sprinkle with grated Parmesan cheese.

With butter, egg, and herbs
Serve asparagus with melted butter, chopped hard-boiled eggs, and finely chopped herbs, such as chives, parsley, chervil, and dill. Goes well with smoked salmon.

With mayonnaise, Parmesan, and lemon
Season mayonnaise with grated Parmesan cheese and lemon juice and serve with asparagus stems. Goes well with air-dried ham.

With fish roe, dill, and sour cream
Stir fish roe and chopped dill into sour cream, and serve with cooked asparagus.

With egg and toast
Serve cooked asparagus stems with creamy scrambled eggs and freshly toasted bread.

With butter and hazelnuts or parsley
Brown butter in a saucepan, then pour it over the asparagus. Sprinkle over chopped hazelnuts or finely chopped parsley.

With butter and vinegar or lemon
Brown butter in a saucepan. Whisk together with the same quantity of softened butter until it is white and airy. Season with a splash of vinegar or lemon juice, salt, and pepper. Store in the fridge but do not let set. Stir before using. Delicious in a sandwich.

See also black salsify tips on page 92.

> **KEEP IN MIND THAT ...**
> the cut surface of the asparagus stems and the tips should be fresh when buying. Cut the stems, as you would for fresh flowers, and place them in a pitcher of cold water, or wrap them in a damp cloth, to make them last longer.

CORN

Corn is the sweetest and juiciest of all vegetables. The cob is enclosed in light green protective leaves and, if recently harvested, can be eaten raw; but it is considerably sweeter when cooked. You can eat corn on the cob whole, sliced, or just the kernels cut from the ear. Stand the cob on a cutting board on its end and hold the top with one hand while cutting straight down with a sharp knife with the other hand. Stir raw corn kernels into salads, soups, and stews. Or cook them in salted water with a pat of butter or cream until soft.

It takes about ten minutes for fresh, whole corn cobs to soften. Use a skewer to check if the corn is tender before serving. You can also steam or broil whole cobs. They can be put directly under the broiler or roasted in the oven. If broiling, avoid burning by parboiling the cobs for a few minutes in a saucepan. Leave the husks on if you want a softer texture, and remove them if you want a chewier consistency. Butter goes very well with cooked, steamed, or broiled corn; you can whisk it until white and fluffy, brown it, or flavor it with lemon, herbs, garlic, or chili.

STORING
Store corn in the fridge, preferably wrapped in a kitchen towel. For longer periods, don't remove the husk. Or cook the cobs for a couple of minutes in salted water, chill in iced water, and refrigerate. Uncooked corn can also be frozen.

SEASON
Fresh corn on the cob is available from mid- to late summer.

GOES WELL WITH
Corn goes well with avocado, tomatoes, bell pepper, lemon, herb, garlic, chili, lemon, bacon, meat, and sausages.

< Corn with chili, garlic, butter, lime, and cilantro.

21 ways of preparing

corn

RAW
Straight up
Enjoy its amazing sweetness and juiciness by eating corn in its purest form.

BOIL
Cook whole
Cook corn cobs in salted water for about 10–15 minutes, or until soft. Pierce with a fork to check if the kernels are soft. Remove, drain, and let cool.

With butter, lemon or lime, and herbs
Whisk softened butter with lemon or lime juice, chopped herbs of your choice, salt, and pepper. Serve the butter with hot corn on the cob.

With butter and chili
Finely chop chilis and combine with soft butter. Spread the chili butter on hot corn on the cobs and season with salt.

With butter, paprika, and cayenne pepper
In a bowl, combine softened butter, paprika, cayenne pepper, and salt. Spread the butter on hot corn on the cobs.

With browned butter
Brown butter in a saucepan. Serve the browned butter with hot corn on the cobs.

With butter and deep-fried garlic
Combine softened butter with deep-fried garlic cloves (see page 132) and season with salt. Spread the butter on hot corn on the cobs.

Cooking corn kernels
Stand the corn on the cob on a cutting board on its end and hold the top with one hand while cutting straight down with a sharp knife with the other, or slant the knife blade in between the rows of kernels and pop them out. Cook in a saucepan of salted water for 3–4 minutes, or until tender. The corn kernels can be frozen raw or blanched. Spread out on a tray and freeze before placing in freezer bags.

With tomato, red onion, garlic, chili, and lime
Cut the kernels from the cob. Cook in a saucepan of salted water for 3–4 minutes, or until soft. Drain. In a bowl, combine the kernels with diced tomatoes, finely chopped red onion, crushed garlic, and chilis. Season with salt, pepper, and lime juice.

With milk, cream, and hard cheese
Cut the kernels from the cob. Cook in a saucepan with equal parts milk and cream for about 5 minutes, or until soft and the liquid has reduced. Stir in grated hard cheese and season with salt and pepper.

With butter and black pepper
Cut the kernels from the cob. Cook in a saucepan of salted water for 3–4 minutes, or until soft. Drain. Add a generous amount of butter and toss to coat. Season with salt and black pepper.

With onion, chicken stock, butter, and parsley
Cut the kernels from the cob. Put into a saucepan with finely chopped onion. Cover with chicken stock and cook until soft. Add a pat of butter and a generous amount of chopped parsley. Season with salt and pepper. Goes well with chicken.

FRY

With flavored butter
Slice corn cobs about 2 inches (5 cm) thick. Cook in a saucepan of salted water. Drain, then fry the slices in a generous amount of butter until they begin to brown. Season with salt and serve with a flavored butter of your choice.

With chili, garlic, lime, and cilantro
Cut the kernels from the cob. Sauté in olive oil with chopped chili and sliced garlic. Add a pat of butter and toss to coat. Season with lime juice and salt, and garnish with chopped cilantro.

With bacon and parsley
Cut the kernels from the cob. Cook cubed bacon in a skillet and add the kernels. Fry until soft, then garnish with chopped parsley.

In salads, stews, and meat sauces
Cut the kernels from the cob. Dry-roast in a skillet until golden brown. Toss corn into a salad, or add to stews or meat sauces.

With sweet chili
Cut kernels from the cob. Dry-roast in a skillet until golden brown. Combine with sweet chili sauce.

With cumin, smoked chili powder, and oregano
Cut kernels from the cob. Sauté in oil until soft. Season with ground cumin, smoked chili powder, oregano, salt, and pepper. Goes well with tortillas.

With black beans, red pepper flakes, white onion or shallot, and cilantro
Cut the kernels from the cob. Cook in a dry skillet until golden brown and transfer to a plate. Add cooked black beans to the saucepan for a few minutes and heat without stirring. Season with dried red pepper flakes, salt, and pepper. Return the kernels to the saucepan with finely chopped onion and shredded cilantro.

ROAST

In the oven
Cut corn cobs into 1-inch (2.5 cm) slices. Toss in olive oil and salt and pepper, and transfer to a baking tray. Roast at 440 °F (220 °C) for about 20–30 minutes, or until soft.

BROIL OR BBQ

To broil
Broiling will be a lot quicker if you cook the corn first. Broil whole cobs or in thicks chunks. Keep the husk on or wrap the corn in aluminum foil, and place directly under the broiler or onto the barbecue. Serve with flavored butter (see page 179).

ONIONS

Yellow onion, red onion, shallot, and white globe onion

Fresh red and green scallions herald the beginning of the onion season. As the young onion isn't fully developed, it doesn't have any peel, its flavor is mild, and its consistency tender. Cook whole or halved in a saucepan of salted water, roast in the oven, or cook under the broiler. You can also serve scallions raw, including the finely chopped or sliced greens. Red onions are particularly attractive in salads, as their flesh has a deep magenta color.

During the fall, the fronds die and are cut off, intensifying the onion's flavor. A protective skin will have developed by now, so that the onion can retain the nutritional goodness it absorbed during the summer.

Cutting an onion unleashes a chemical process, which causes your eyes to water and your nose to run. You can reduce the irritation by storing onions in the fridge and cutting them with a very sharp knife. The more finely you chop an onion, the stronger the flavor and aroma that are released. However, the chemicals which produce the tears are also the ones that give the onion its wonderfully pungent flavor.

Raw chopped or sliced onion oxidizes quickly, so you should use it immediately after chopping.

Leek and scallion

Leeks may look quite different from onions, but they belong to the same family. Leeks are milder and not as sweet as onions. Use the entire leek—raw or cooked, even the small roots have an intense flavor. The pale part is the mildest. Cut along the entire leek and rinse thoroughly with water to remove any sand and grit.

Scallions look like small leeks and are mild and pleasant raw, boiled, fried, or broiled.

Garlic

Garlic is available newly harvested in spring. Because it is relatively mild in flavor, it can be eaten raw. Cut it into thin slices and add to a salad, or scatter over fried potatoes.

Fresh garlic, with visible cloves whose peel hasn't dried yet, is comparatively mild and very good roasted whole in the oven. Older garlic cloves tend to sprout and it's best to remove these sprouts, which may also indicate the garlic has not been stored well.

Garlic becomes sweeter if you cook the cloves for a long time, roast them in the oven, or blanch before cooking. You can easily crush or slice a garlic clove. Finely chopped garlic will be strong in flavor, and crushed garlic even stronger. Wait for the right moment to add garlic to a skillet; burnt garlic tastes bitter.

STORING
The vegetable drawer at the bottom of the fridge is good for keeping yellow onions, red onions, shallots, and white globe onions. Place them in a paper bag as they are sensitive to humidity. Onions will sprout and soften more quickly at room temperature. Fresh yellow onions, red onions, as well as leeks and scallions should be stored in a cool, dark place.

SEASON
Onions are a cold-season crop grown over the winter in milder climates, and available year-round as an imported crop. They can be stored in a root cellar.

GOES WELL WITH
Yellow onion, red onion, shallot, white globe onion, and garlic go well with almost everything. Leek and scallion go especially well with bacon, smoked ham, fish, cream, and potatoes.

From the left: deep-fried garlic; small onion with white wine, rosemary or thyme, honey, and lemon; pickled red onion and fried scallion with lemon.

Yellow onion has a sharp flavor, which converts to a lovely sweetness when cooked. Even the consistency changes: from crispy when raw to soft and juicy when cooked. Yellow onion is usually cooked, broiled, deep-fried, or sautéed. Fry over a high heat for a few minutes and lower the temperature when the onion begins to soften.

Red onion has a milder taste than yellow onion and can be used raw. It can also be cooked.

Shallot has always been a popular ingredient. It is mild and incredibly tasty raw, finely chopped in vinaigrette, or thinly sliced in a tomato salad. Use in dishes where the flavor of a yellow onion would be too strong.

White globe onion is very mild and can be eaten raw. Thanks to its small size, it's easier to peel and chop than other onions or shallots. As round as a yellow onion but with a white, almost silvery peel, this onion is completely white. And in contrast to a red onion, it won't color other ingredients.

20 ways of preparing yellow onion, red onion, shallot & white globe onion

RAW
Red onion with lemon and honey
Thinly sliced red onion has a milder flavor if briefly placed in iced water. Drain and combine with salt, lemon juice, and honey.

Red onion with vinegar
Thinly slice red onion and place in a bowl. Whisk together 1 part white wine vinegar, 3 parts oil, salt, and pepper. Cover onion with the vinaigrette and let stand for 5–10 minutes.

Shallot in vinaigrette
Finely chop shallots and place in a bowl. Whisk together with 1 part red wine vinegar, 3 parts olive oil, salt, and pepper in a bowl. Add chopped fresh herbs, such as tarragon, dill, or parsley. This is a good basic vinaigrette.

White globe onion with cilantro and lime
Finely chop white globe onion. Place in a bowl and combine with chopped cilantro and lemon juice. Goes well with tacos and other Mexican-style foods.

PICKLE
Red onion, white globe onion, or shallot, vinegar, and sugar
Boil 1 part vinegar, 2 parts white sugar, 3 parts water, and some salt in a saucepan. Let cool slightly. Slice onion and place in a bowl. Cover with the hot liquid and let stand for at least 30 minutes. Covered with plastic wrap, it will keep for about one week in the fridge. The onion tends to wilt the longer it is in the vinegar.

BOIL
Shallot with soy
Finely chop shallots and sauté in olive oil until soft, without browning. Add a dash of light soy sauce and heat through. Goes well with fish.

Yellow onion with garlic, thyme, bay leaves, white wine, and stock
Slice yellow onion and garlic and sauté in a skillet with oil, thyme, and bay leaves. Add a dash of white wine, bring to the boil, and simmer for a few minutes. Cover with stock and cook until soft. Season with salt and pepper. An easy-to-make onion soup.

White globe onion, garlic, white wine, stock, crème fraîche, and chive
Slice white globe onion and garlic and sauté in a skillet with butter until soft. Don't allow the onion to brown. Add a dash of white wine and bring to the boil, then simmer for a few minutes. Cover with stock and cook for a further 15 minutes. Stir in a spoonful of crème fraîche. Season with salt and pepper, and sprinkle with chopped chives.

White globe onion with garlic, sugar, lemon, and herbs

Finely chop white globe onion and garlic and cook in olive oil until soft. Sprinkle with raw cane sugar and grated lemon zest. Continue cooking until it develops a jam-like consistency. Season with salt, pepper, lemon juice and, if liked, chopped herbs. Mint would be ideal if the onion jam is to be served with lamb, and thyme if it is to be served with fish, pork, or beef. Serve the jam hot or at room temperature.

FRY
For children who do not like onion

If your children don't like onions, here's a good tip. Roughly chop and gently sauté onion in butter without browning it. Purée it, adding a little oil if it is too thick. Use this onion cream in all types of dishes. Make a large batch and freeze in smaller portions. This way, the onion is much milder than chopped or sliced raw, plus it is not visible in the dish.

Small onion with white wine, rosemary or thyme, honey, and lemon

Peel small onions and brown them whole in a saucepan with butter. Cover with white wine, scatter with rosemary or thyme, and bring to the boil. Cook until the liquid has evaporated and the onions are soft. Stir in honey and season with grated lemon zest, salt, and pepper. Goes well with beef or roasted cabbage.

Yellow onion with garlic, butter, and beer

Finely chop yellow onion and fry in oil over a medium heat. Don't stir too much or let the onion brown. Add chopped garlic and a generous pat of butter and sauté for a few minutes more. Add beer and cook. Season with salt. Goes well with Salisbury steak.

Onion with lemon, olive oil, and honey

Cut any onion into thick wedges. In a bowl, whisk together 1 part lemon juice, 2 parts olive oil, and honey. Cover onion with the marinade and let stand for a few minutes. Sauté in a skillet with a pat of butter until soft and golden brown. Season with salt and pepper. Goes well with fish.

White globe onion with sugar and beer or white wine

Thinly slice white globe onion and sauté in a skillet with a generous pat of butter, until soft and golden brown. Sprinkle with sugar and sauté until the onion caramelizes. Pour in a dash of beer or white wine and bring to the boil. Season with salt and pepper. Goes well with burgers.

Yellow onion with cream

Slice yellow onion and sauté in a skillet with butter until golden brown. Add cream and bring to the boil; this makes a lovely creamy sauce.

ROAST
Small onion with Parmesan

On a plate or in an ovenproof dish, coat small onion halves in olive oil and season with salt and pepper. Season with salt and pepper. Roast at 300 °F (150 °C) for 20–30 minutes, or until soft. Top with grated Parmesan cheese.

Any onion with thyme

Place onion wedges on a baking tray. Coat with olive oil, and add thyme, salt, and pepper. Roast at 400 °F (200 °C) for 15–20 minutes, or until soft and golden brown.

Any whole unpeeled onion

Place whole unpeeled onions on a baking tray and roast at 150 °F (75 °C) for about 45 minutes. Cut onions in half and remove the peel. Serve with salt, pepper, and a pat of butter. Or heat in a skillet together with butter and thin apple wedges. Goes well with fish.

BROIL
Any onion with butter and pepper

Place a whole unpeeled onion under the broiler and cook for about 20 minutes, or until it has softened. Peel the onion, cut a cross in the top, and place on a plate. Mix softened butter with salt and coarsely ground pepper. Place a pat of butter onto the cross in the top of the onion and serve hot.

DEEP-FRY
Yellow onion with flour or cornstarch
Peel a yellow onion and cut into very thin and even slices. Coat in plenty of all-purpose flour or cornstarch in a bowl. Shake off the excess and deep-fry, a few onion rings, at a time in hot oil. Drain on paper towels. Sprinkle with salt.

11 ways of preparing leek & scallion

BOIL
Leek with cream, tomato, and dill
Cook cream in a saucepan and reduce by half. Add sliced leek and diced tomatoes and cook for a couple of minutes. Combine with a generous amount of chopped dill and season with salt and pepper. Goes well with fried fish.

Leek with stock, butter, mayonnaise, Dijon mustard, and croutons
Simmer vegetable stock in a saucepan with a lid, and add 1-inch (2.5 cm) pieces of leek with a pat of butter. Put on the lid and simmer until soft. Remove the leek and place on a plate. In a bowl, flavor mayonnaise with wholegrain Dijon mustard. Coat the leeks with the mayonnaise, season with salt and pepper, and add croutons.

Leek with potato and crème fraîche
Slice leek and potato, then fry in oil in a saucepan for a few minutes. Cover with stock and cook until soft. Blend to make a soup and then dilute with extra stock until you have the desired consistency. Whisk in a spoonful of crème fraîche and season with salt and pepper.

FRY
Leek in pieces
Cut leeks into 4-inch (10 cm) chunks and cook in a saucepan of salted water for about 5 minutes, or until soft. Remove and place in a bowl of iced water. Drain. Sauté in butter until the leeks begins to color. Season with salt and pepper. Halve each piece lengthwise and serve.

Leek with spinach
Thinly slice leeks and sauté in butter until soft. Add shredded spinach and cook for a few minutes more. Season with salt and pepper. Goes well with fish.

Scallion with lemon
Sauté a whole scallion in oil until soft. Season with grated lemon zest, lemon juice, salt, and pepper.

Scallion with goat cheese, crème fraîche, honey, and tomato
In a bowl, combine equal parts of goat cheese and crème fraîche. Season with honey, salt, and pepper. Sauté a whole scallion in oil for a few minutes, then transfer to a plate. Place tomato halves, cut surface down, in the same skillet and fry for 3–4 minutes. Transfer them to the plate. Serve with the goat cheese mixture.

ROAST/BAKE
Leek with thyme, butter, pork, and cheese
Arrange 1-inch (2.5 cm) leek slices on a baking tray with fresh thyme, salt, and pepper. Spread with softened butter. Roast at 300 °F (150 °C) for 20 minutes, or until soft. Remove and scatter with cubed cooked pork and grated cheese.

In puff pastry with leek, walnuts, and cheese
Sliced leeks and sauté in olive oil until they start to turn golden. Add chopped walnuts. Transfer a thin layer of the mixture to small squares of pastry and top with a piece of cheese. Pinch the edges together. Bake at 400 °F (200 °C) until the pastry has risen and turned golden brown.

BROIL
Leek with olive oil
Rinse, dry, and place a leek under the broiler. Broil until the leek is almost entirely black. Remove the outer leaves and cut the leek into slices. Place on a plate, and dress with olive oil, salt, and pepper.

Scallion with lemon
Toss a whole scallion in oil and broil until soft. Place on a plate and squeeze over lemon juice. Season with salt and pepper.

< Leek with thyme, butter, pork, and cheese.

9 ways of preparing garlic

RAW
With salad or potato
Early season garlic tastes delicious raw. Thinly slice and toss in a salad, or serve with cooked or fried potatoes.

With oil
Peel the garlic cloves, cover with olive oil, and toss. Use to brush onto fish, meat, chicken, or vegetables before frying or broiling.

With butter and bread
In a bowl, stir crushed garlic into softened butter. Spread onto slices of bread and toast at 400 °F (200 °C) until golden brown.

With parsley, lemon, and olive oil
In a bowl, combine chopped garlic and parsley with grated lemon zest and olive oil. Goes well with fish.

BOIL
With butter and thyme
Melt a generous pat of butter in a small saucepan. Add unpeeled garlic cloves and thyme, and simmer until soft. Serve with eggplant or lamb.

With butter, olive oil, and anchovies
Thinly slice garlic and simmer in a saucepan over a low heat in equal parts butter and olive oil with chopped anchovies for 5–7 minutes. Pour over cooked vegetables.

FRY
With dried red pepper flakes
Sauté crushed garlic cloves and dried red pepper flakes in a skillet with oil for a few minutes before adding the flavored oil to fish, vegetables, or chicken.

ROAST
With white wine, olive oil, and thyme
Cut off the top of a bulb of garlic and place on a baking tray. Drizzle with white wine and olive oil and season with salt and fresh thyme. Bake at 400 °F (200 °C) for about 20–30 minutes, or until the garlic cloves are soft and start peeking through the skin.

DEEP-FRY
In oil
Deep-fry thinly sliced garlic in hot oil until golden brown and drain on paper towels. Drizzle over cooked vegetables or use to season mashed potato or mayonnaise.

Garlic with white wine, olive oil, and thyme. >

FENNEL

Fennel is a member of the carrot family, and is related to dill and parsley. The leaves are full of flavor and can be served fresh or dried, used as a seasoning or as a garnish. Fennel seeds can also be used as seasoning. However, it is best known for its bulb which is eaten raw or cooked.

To trim fennel, cut off the stems. They are usually too hard to eat raw and require a longer cooking time than the bulb and fronds. However, sliced fennel stems are excellent in slow-cooked dishes, such as stewed vegetables and fish stock. Trim any brown stains from the outer layer with a potato peeler or a knife. Cut the fennel bulb in half and trim off the coarse end if the fennel is not young and tender.

Thinly slice the bulb halves with a mandolin slicer or a sharp knife. If you want to eat the fennel raw, place the slices in iced water for a few minutes so they remain crisp. If you would rather eat them cooked—boiled, fried, roasted or broiled—prepare in whichever way works best for the dish: in wedges, sliced, or chopped into large or small cubes.

Thinly sliced fennel can be sautéed. Larger slices can be blanched before being sautéed or baked. Otherwise, the fennel's texture might become chewy and hard.

STORING
Store fennel wrapped in a kitchen towel in the fridge.

SEASON
Fennel is planted after the last spring frost and can be harvested through summer and fall. Because it is very frost sensitive, the season can end abruptly.

GOES WELL WITH
Fennel goes well with tomatoes, cucumber, lemon, pear, fish, parsley, dill, olive, saffron, cheese, and seafood.

Fennel with stock, garlic, orange, olive, and basil. >

21 ways of preparing fennel

RAW
Prepared
Cut the stems from the bulb and remove any brown areas. Halve, then trim off the rough ends. Thinly slice or grate to serve.

With anchovies, orange, olive, and vinaigrette
In a bowl, combine thinly sliced fennel, chopped anchovies, orange segments, and olives. Whisk together 1 part red wine vinegar, 3 parts olive oil, salt, and pepper. Toss the salad with the vinaigrette and let stand for a few minutes to allow the flavors to mature.

With red onion, lemon, dill, and snow peas
In a bowl, combine thinly sliced fennel and red onion. Season with grated lemon zest, lemon juice, chopped dill, salt, pepper, and a dash of olive oil. Add some raw snow peas if liked.

With capers, dill, mayonnaise, crème fraîche, and lemon
In a bowl, combine thinly sliced fennel, capers, and chopped dill. Combine with equal parts mayonnaise and crème fraîche. Season with lemon juice, salt, and pepper.

With rhubarb, dill, and lemon
In a bowl, combine thinly sliced fennel bulb, rhubarb, and chopped dill. Whisk together 1 part lemon juice, 2 parts oil, salt, pepper and a pinch of sugar in a large bowl. Toss the vegetables in the dressing. Goes well with chicken, or broiled vegetables.

With potato, scallion, vinaigrette, and dill
In a bowl, combine thinly sliced fennel, sliced cold cooked potatoes, and scallions. Whisk together 1 part white wine vinegar with 2 parts oil. Toss the salad with the vinaigrette. Season with salt and pepper, and sprinkle with plenty of chopped dill.

With leek, potato, tarragon, and vinaigrette
Slice fennel on a mandolin slicer, then combine in a bowl with thinly sliced leek, cold cooked potato slices, and finely chopped tarragon. Whisk together 1 part vinegar, 2 parts olive oil, salt, and pepper. Add the vinaigrette to the bowl.

PICKLE
With vinegar, sugar, water, and parsley
Thinly slice fennel and put into a preserving jar with a lid. Bring 1 part vinegar, 2 parts sugar, and 3 parts water to the boil. Let cool. Pour over the fennel and let stand for a few hours. Remove the fennel from the jar and combine with chopped parsley. Goes well with fried fish. Store in the fridge for up to two weeks.

BOIL
With butter and basil
Chop fennel and cook in a saucepan of salted water until soft. Drain the water and add a pat of butter and shredded basil to the saucepan. Season with salt and pepper.

With stock, garlic, orange, olive, and basil
Cut fennel into wedges, place in a saucepan, and cover with vegetable stock. Add chopped garlic, orange zest, and orange juice. Cook until the fennel is soft, remove and in a bowl combine with black olives and shredded basil. Bring the stock back to the boil and whisk in a dash of olive oil, a pat of butter, salt, and pepper. Serve with the stock. Goes well with fish.

With onion, garlic, saffron, white wine, and stock
Cut fennel into wedges. Sauté chopped onion and garlic in olive oil in a saucepan over a low heat. Add saffron. When the onion becomes transparent, add the fennel. Cover with equal parts white wine and stock, salt and pepper. Simmer for about 30 minutes, or until soft.

With cream and dill
Sliced fennel and sauté in a saucepan with butter. Cover with cream, and add a generous amount of chopped dill. Cook until soft and the cream has thickened. Season with salt and pepper. Goes well with fish.

With cream, tomato, red onion, and dill
Pour cream into a saucepan, bring to the boil, and then simmer until reduced to one-third. Thinly slice fennel and stir into the cream and cook for a few minutes. Stir into a bowl with halved cherry tomatoes, sliced red onion, and chopped dill. Season with salt and pepper.

With onion, garlic, lemon, white wine, vegetable stock, crème fraîche, and basil
Sliced fennel and sauté in a skillet with olive oil, coarsely chopped onion, and garlic. Add lemon zest and cover with a dash of white wine, and vegetable stock. Cook until tender. Drain and reserve the liquid. Blend the vegetables to make a smooth soup, adding the reserved liquid until it is the desired consistency. Stir in crème fraîche for a creamier soup. Heat and season with shredded basil, salt, and pepper.

With scallion, garlic, mussels, white wine, and cream
Dice fennel and sauté in a saucepan with olive oil, chopped scallion, and garlic. Do not let the ingredients brown. Add mussels. Pour in a generous amount of white wine and some cream. Cover and simmer until the mussels have opened, about 5 minutes. Season with salt and, if desired, chopped garlic.

In tomato sauce
Add diced fennel to tomato sauce at the end of the cooking time. Goes well with fish.

> **THE TASTE OF LICORICE**
> Fennel's signature licorice flavor is sharp and fresh when raw. It is diminished when boiled, and gets stronger when the sugar in the fennel is caramelized during frying.

In fish soup
Add thinly sliced fennel to fish soup at the end of the cooking time.

With lemon
The flavor of fennel is less pronounced when you slowly fry slices in butter and olive oil. Season with lemon juice, salt, and pepper.

With onion, tarragon, and cherry tomato
Chop fennel and sauté in olive oil until soft. Add finely chopped onion, plenty of chopped tarragon, and halved cherry tomatoes. Season with salt and pepper, and toss to combine. Goes well with fish.

ROAST
With Parmesan
Cook fennel wedges in a saucepan of salted water for a few minutes. Drain, toss in olive oil, and roast at 400 °F (200 °C) for about 15 minutes, or until soft. Scatter with grated Parmesan cheese and roast for a few more minutes.

In a potato gratin with dill
Add a layer of thinly sliced fennel to the potato slices in a potato gratin. Sprinkle with plenty of chopped dill.

KOHLRABI

Kohlrabi is one of the most unusual vegetables to look at, and its strange appearance might be one of the reasons why it is often ignored. However, underneath that knobbly shape is a very delicious root. Kohlrabi grows rapidly and should be harvested before it becomes too big. Once the bulb has started aging, the flavor becomes woody and the texture fibrous. A normal-sized kohlrabi weighs just under 1 pound (450 g) and grows between 3–4 inches (7–10 cm) long. Recently introduced varieties remain tender even when large and mature.

Kohlrabi has white flesh which is crispy and succulent, and has a mild taste reminiscent of cauliflower, cabbage, and turnip. In most cases, the peel is so thick that it should be removed. Many cooks believe kohlrabi should be eaten raw, thinly sliced or grated into a salad. Others enjoy it cooked and tossed in butter. Kohlrabi also goes well in soups and stews, fried or roasted, on its own or with other vegetables. If you are lucky enough to find kohlrabi with leaves, you can eat those raw, steamed, or pan-fried.

STORING
Store kohlrabi in the fridge, preferably wrapped in a damp towel.

SEASON
Kohlrabi is planted several weeks before the last frost in spring, or in late summer for winter harvest. It is cold-tolerant, but will not grow well in extremely hot climates.

GOES WELL WITH
Kohlrabi goes well with mustard, lemon, apple, pear, herbs, horseradish, nuts, curry, vinegar, butter, cream, fish, smoked meat, and bacon.

Kohlrabi with red onion, pear, vinaigrette, honey, and almonds. >

12 ways of preparing kohlrabi

RAW
With apple, walnuts, and vinaigrette
Peel and coarsely grate kohlrabi. Combine in a bowl with chopped walnuts. Whisk together 1 part apple cider vinegar, 3 parts oil, salt, and pepper. Pour the vinaigrette into the bowl.

With apple, leek, yogurt, and honey
Peel and coarsely grate kohlrabi. Combine in a bowl with grated apple and sliced leek. In a separate bowl, combine thick yogurt with honey, salt, and pepper. Stir into the kohlrabi.

With carrot, parsley, cumin, and lemon
Peel and coarsely grate kohlrabi. Combine in a bowl with thinly sliced carrot and chopped parsley. Toast whole cumin seeds in a dry skillet and add to the bowl. Season with lemon juice, olive oil, salt, and pepper.

With red onion, pear, vinaigrette, honey, and almonds
Peel and thinly slice kohlrabi. Combine in a bowl with sliced red onion and thinly sliced pear wedges. Whisk together 1 part white wine vinegar, 3 parts olive oil, honey, salt, and pepper. Pour the vinaigrette into the bowl. Garnish with roasted almonds. Goes well with cold cuts.

With shallot, parsley, mustard, and vinaigrette
Peel kohlrabi and cut into strips. Combine in a bowl with sliced shallots and finely chopped parsley. Whisk together 1 part whole grain Dijon mustard, 1 part vinegar, 3 parts oil, salt, and pepper. Stir the vinaigrette into the bowl.

With dip
Peel and cut kohlrabi strips. Serve with a dip (see pages 177–178).

BOIL
With butter, chive, and lemon
Chop kohlrabi and cook in a saucepan of salted water until soft. Drain and add a pat of butter and finely cut chives. Season with lemon juice, salt, and pepper.

With crème fraîche, mustard, and chive or dill
Chop kohlrabi and cook in a saucepan of salted water until soft. Drain and add crème fraîche. Season with Dijon mustard, white pepper, and chopped chives or dill. Goes well with fish.

With yellow onion, vinegar, apple, cashews, and romaine lettuce
Thinly slice kohlrabi and yellow onions and sauté in olive oil in a saucepan. Season with a dash of red wine vinegar, salt, and pepper. Fold in diced apple, cashews, and coarsely chopped romaine lettuce.

With garlic, chili, and cilantro
Peel and slice kohlrabi, then cook in a saucepan of salted water. Drain and let cool. Sauté in a skillet with chopped garlic, chili, and olive oil. Sprinkle with cilantro.

FRY
With garlic, spinach, or chard
Peel and cube kohlrabi, then sauté in a skillet with olive oil, a pat of butter, and garlic. Spread over chopped spinach or chard. Season with salt and pepper.

ROAST
With new potato, garlic, and lemon
Peel and chop kohlrabi, then combine with scrubbed, equal-sized new potatoes in a baking tray. Toss in olive oil, chopped garlic, and grated lemon zest. Roast at 400 °F (200 °C) for about 20–30 minutes, or until soft.

CELERY

The color, flavor, and consistency of celery stalks depend on their variety. The stalks can be soft and mild or have a more distinctive, bitter taste. They range in color from nearly white to medium green. It's wise to taste celery before using it in a recipe and adjust the amount according to its depth of flavor. Generally, the darker the color, the stronger the flavor.

The crisp stalks are ideal served raw in salads or with dips, or cooked in sauces, casseroles, and soups together with onion and carrots (this trio is often known as mirepoix). Dice the three ingredients and fry gently in olive oil or butter until soft before adding any liquid. Make an extra-large quantity of mirepoix and freeze. It's a great base for all kinds of soups.

If the celery still has its leaves attached, they can be used as a herb to add depth to a soup or stew, or chopped and added to a green salad. The leaves can also be dried in a low oven, then pulsed in a food processor with salt to create homemade celery salt. Use in soups and stews.

STORING
Store celery wrapped in a kitchen towel in the fridge. Wrap wilted celery in damp paper towels before placing in the fridge. Or cut into cubes and sauté in oil, preferably with carrots and yellow onion, and freeze.

SEASON
Celery is grown from mid- to late spring into summer. Extreme heat will cause it to bolt. It is also cultivated year-round in greenhouses.

GOES WELL WITH
Celery goes well with tomatoes, carrots, lemon, apple, pear, onion, garlic, lentils, nuts, soy, vinegar, stock, blue cheese, fish, and bacon.

20 ways of preparing celery

RAW

With soy and lemon
Thinly slice celery and place in a bowl. Whisk together 1 part light soy sauce with 1 part lemon juice. Pour the marinade into the bowl and let stand. Goes well with fried fish.

With tomato, leek, lentils, mustard, vinaigrette, and chive
Thinly slice or shave celery. In a bowl, combine celery with sliced tomato, leek, and cooked lentils. Whisk together 1 part Dijon mustard, 1 part vinegar, 3 parts olive oil, chopped chives, salt, and pepper. Use to dress the celery salad. Goes well with chicken.

With leek, vinaigrette, and lettuce
Thinly slice equal amounts of celery and leek, and combine on a bowl. Whisk together 1 part white wine vinegar, 3 parts olive oil, salt, and pepper. Toss the celery and leek with the vinaigrette. Add lettuce and toss again.

With red onion, tomato, and vinaigrette
Thinly slice celery and red onion, and dice tomatoes. Combine in a bowl. Whisk together 1 part vinegar, 3 parts olive oil, salt, and pepper. Toss the vegetables with the vinaigrette.

With pear, walnuts, vinaigrette, and honey or goat cheese
Thinly slice celery and pears. Combine in a bowl with roasted, chopped walnuts. Whisk together 1 part vinegar, 3 parts olive oil, salt, and pepper. Toss the celery and pears with the vinaigrette. Serve the salad drizzled with some honey or crumble goat cheese over the top.

With mushrooms, red onion, herbs, mayonnaise, and croutons
Thinly slice celery and mushrooms, and combine with finely chopped red onion in a bowl. Stir finely chopped herbs into mayonnaise and season with salt and pepper. Spoon the mayonnaise dressing over the vegetables and top with croutons.

With apple, lemon, honey, and hazelnuts
Cut celery into cubes and combine with shredded apple. Squeeze lemon juice over the top, and add honey and coarsely chopped hazelnuts. Serve the salad with a mature blue-veined cheese or goat cheese and toast.

With tomato juice and hot sauce
In a bowl, combine chopped celery with tomato juice and season with a few dashes of hot sauce. The celery will take some of the heat out of the hot sauce.

With rye bread, ricotta, and herbs
Place slices of rye bread on a baking tray. Toast at 300 °F (150 °C) until crisp. Grate or pulse the bread to make crumbs. Combine ricotta cheese with coarsely chopped herbs to make a smooth cream. Season with salt and pepper. Cut celery into sticks and dip first into the cheese and then the breadcrumbs.

With lemon dressing
Very thinly slice celery and place in a bowl. Whisk together 1 part lemon juice, 2 parts oil, salt, and pepper. Toss the celery with the dressing. Serve with fish or salad.

With tapenade and cured ham
Cut celery into sticks. Spread tapenade onto thin slices of cured ham. Place a couple of celery sticks on top and roll up.

With tomato, white beans, basil, and vinaigrette
Cut celery into cubes. In a bowl, combine with chopped tomatoes, cooked white beans, and shredded basil. Whisk together 1 part vinegar, 3 parts olive oil, salt, and pepper. Toss the salad with the vinaigrette. Goes well with baked eggplant.

Celery with tomato, leek, lentils, mustard, vinaigrette, and chive. >

BOIL

With yellow onion, carrot, garlic, stock, and other vegetables

For an easy-to-make vegetable soup, chop equal amounts of celery, yellow onion, and carrot. Sauté in olive oil with chopped garlic. Add stock, chopped vegetables of your choice, and simmer until the vegetables are tender.

With cucumber, cherry tomato, and dill

Slice celery and put into a saucepan. Add seeded cucumber, halved cherry tomatoes, and olive oil and cook over a medium heat. Season with salt and pepper and garnish with chopped dill. Goes well with fish.

With celery root, leek, and butter

Slice celery, celery root, and leek. Put into a saucepan of salted water and bring to the boil. Drain and add a pat of butter. Season with salt and pepper. Goes well with fish.

With garlic, yellow onion, stock, vinegar, butter, and parsley

Chop celery, garlic, and yellow onion and place in a saucepan. Barely cover with vegetable stock. Add a dash of red wine vinegar, a tablespoon of butter, and pepper. Simmer for about 30 minutes, or until the vegetables are soft. Spoon onto soup plates and garnish with a generous amount of chopped parsley.

FRY

With onion, honey, vinegar, and herbs

Slice celery and onion and sauté in butter. Toss with honey, a dash of vinegar, salt, and pepper. Garnish with fresh herbs of your choice. Goes well with goat cheese.

With olive and cherry tomato

Cut celery into chunks and lightly sauté in olive oil. Remove the celery when it begins to brown. Add pitted olives and halved cherry tomatoes. Season with salt and pepper. Goes well with baked fish.

ROAST

With lemon and bacon or pancetta

Chop celery, toss with olive oil and lemon juice, and arrange on a baking tray. Dot with cubed bacon or pancetta and season with salt. Roast at 400 °F (200 °C) for about 20 minutes, or until soft.

With red onion, apple, thyme, and butter

Chop celery and place on a sheet of aluminum foil. Top with thinly sliced red onion, apple wedges, a generous amount of thyme, and two tablespoons of butter. Season with salt and pepper and fold over to seal. Roast at 350 °F (175 °C) for about 15 minutes, or until the celery is soft. Goes well with broiled pork chops.

BEANS

Green bean, yellow wax bean, velour bean, string bean

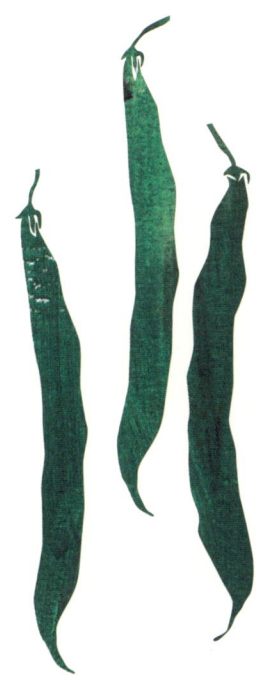

Green, yellow wax, velour, and string beans are four types of garden beans that can all be prepared in very similar ways and share the same flavor, although string beans usually have a slightly more intense taste. String and green beans are the same green color, while the wax bean is yellow, and the velour bean is naturally dark purple, but will turn green when cooked.

The garden beans are usually cooked. Start by trimming them. Snap or cut off the stem end and steam, boil, or sauté the beans either whole or in slices. Cook over a medium heat in a saucepan to ensure the beans become soft before they burn. The beans can be blanched in salted water for a few minutes, then drained and fried quickly in oil over a high heat.

When warm, the beans are perfect with just a pat of butter. Or they can be chilled in iced water and folded into mixed salads.

Buy plentiful fresh beans in season. Blanch and freeze for later, or freeze the raw beans. They can be cooked from frozen and served as a side dish.

STORING
Store green, yellow wax, velour, and string beans wrapped in a kitchen towel in the fridge. Blanched beans can be stored in the freezer.

SEASON
Beans are grown from late spring into summer, and can also be grown in fall. Because they are very frost sensitive, the season can end abruptly.

GOES WELL WITH
Beans go well with tomatoes, arugula, mushrooms, lemon, herbs, onion, garlic, chili, ginger, capers, nuts, light soy sauce, vinegar, butter, anchovies, and bacon.

21 ways of preparing beans

BOIL
Trim and boil
Trim beans by snapping off the stem. Cook them whole, or cut in small, diagonal slices, in a saucepan of salted water, for about 5 minutes. They should be soft but have a little crunch left. Beans can be blanched and frozen. Spread them on a tray and partly freeze them before placing in freezer bags.

With butter or olive oil and lemon juice
In a bowl, toss cooked beans with a pat of butter or olive oil and lemon juice. Season with salt and pepper and serve with mayonnaise.

With lemon, garlic, and dried red pepper flakes
In a bowl, toss cooked beans with lemon juice, finely chopped garlic, and dried red pepper flakes.

With butter, almonds, and lemon juice
Place cooked beans in a dish. Brown chopped almonds in butter in a skillet for a couple of minutes over a low heat. Remove from the heat and add lemon juice. Pour the butter and almonds over the beans.

With onion and capers
Place cooked beans in a dish. Sauté finely chopped onion in butter until soft. Add capers, and pour the mixture over the beans. Season with salt and pepper.

With tomato, red onion, olive, basil, and vinaigrette
In a bowl, combine cooked beans, sliced tomatoes, chopped red onion, chopped olives, and basil. Whisk together 1 part vinegar, 3 parts olive oil, salt, and pepper. Toss the vegetables in the vinaigrette. Goes well with fish or chicken.

With vinaigrette, prosciutto, and croutons
Put hot or cold cooked beans into a bowl. Whisk together 1 part balsamic vinegar, 3 parts olive oil, salt and pepper. Toss beans with the vinaigrette and top with crisply fried diced prosciutto and croutons.

With yogurt and lemon
In a bowl, combine cold cooked beans with thick yogurt. Season with grated lemon zest, salt, and pepper.

With shrimps, dill, and vinaigrette
In a bowl, combine cooked beans, shrimp, and chopped dill. Whisk together 2 parts lemon juice, 2 parts olive oil, salt, and pepper. Toss the beans and shrimp with the vinaigrette. Goes well with roasted cauliflower.

With cream, shallot, and dill
Cook cream until reduced and thickened. Combine cooked beans, finely chopped shallots, and dill, and add to the cream. Serve warm or cold. Goes well with fish.

With shallot, dill, salmon, and lemon juice
In a bowl, combine cooked beans, thinly sliced shallots and chopped dill. Add chopped smoked salmon. Season with salt, pepper, and lemon juice. Works well as a topping on slices of sourdough bread.

FRY
With lemon juice and dill
Sauté raw or parboiled beans in olive oil until soft. Season with lemon juice, chopped dill, salt, and pepper.

With garlic, parsley, and anchovies
Place cooked beans in a dish. Sauté chopped garlic, parsley, and anchovies in olive oil for a couple of minutes. Spread over the beans. Season with pepper

Green and yellow wax beans with chili, ginger, and soy sauce. >

With red onion, garlic, and Parmesan

Sauté raw or parboiled beans in olive oil with thinly sliced red onion and finely chopped garlic. Season with salt and pepper, and top with grated Parmesan cheese.

With chili, ginger, and soy sauce

Sauté raw or parboiled beans in olive oil with finely chopped chilis and peeled and sliced ginger until soft. Season with a dash of light soy sauce, salt, and pepper. Goes well with broiled salmon or beef.

With garlic, sesame, mayonnaise, and soy sauce

Sauté raw or parboiled beans in olive oil with sliced garlic until soft. Sprinkle with sesame seeds, salt, and pepper, and transfer to a plate. Flavor mayonnaise with light soy sauce. Serve the beans with the mayonnaise.

With bacon

Fry cubed bacon in a skillet. When the bacon begins to crisp, add cooked beans and fry for a couple of minutes.

With pork belly, mushrooms, garlic, and parsley

Sauté raw or parboiled beans in butter with cubed smoked pork belly and sliced mushrooms for a few minutes, or until soft. Add crushed garlic, finely chopped parsley, salt, and pepper.

With garlic, vinegar, and parsley

Sauté sliced garlic in olive oil. Add cooked beans and cook until they take on a little color. Season with a dash of red wine vinegar, chopped parsley, salt, and pepper.

BROIL

Smoky

Cover the broiler with a large sheet of aluminum foil. Spread trimmed beans over the foil and broil until they begin to brown. Toss with olive oil and sea salt.

DEEP-FRY

With tempura batter, mayonnaise, soy sauce, and sriracha or sesame

Snap off the stem ends of the beans. Cook in salted water until soft and then drain. Dip the beans into tempura batter. Deep-fry in hot oil until golden brown, and drain on paper towels. Serve with mayonnaise flavored with light soy sauce, sriracha, or roasted sesame seeds.

AVOCADO

Avocados have increased in popularity recently due to their amazing flavor, velvety texture, beautiful color, versatility, and health benefits.

The perfect, ready-to-eat avocado is firm, with just a little give, but not squishy. As finding it can be a challenge, it's often easiest to buy slightly hard avocados and ripen them at home. Leave to stand at room temperature for quicker ripening, or store in the fridge, which will take slightly longer. Avocados ripen at different speeds, so check regularly on their progress!

Avocados are usually eaten raw—a ripe avocado melts in the mouth like butter. Less than perfectly ripe avocados can be thinly sliced into an omelet or salad, or drizzled with oil and lemon juice and gently broiled.

To prepare avocados, first cut in half lengthwise, from stem to base. To remove the stone, ease out with a spoon or very carefully using a sharp knife. Slice or cut the flesh in a grid and scoop out with the spoon. Avocados oxidize quickly, so brush the flesh with lemon juice. If preparing guacamole, prevent it from browning by placing the stone in the bowl and covering it tightly with plastic wrap.

STORING
Store the avocado in the vegetable drawer of the fridge where it is the least cool. Freeze avocado by cutting in half, removing the stone, and placing in freezer bags.

SEASON
Avocado is harvested in countries with consistently warm climates throughout summer. Be sure to buy organic avocados that should be allowed to ripen at home.

GOES WELL WITH
Avocado goes well with citrus fruit, mango, herbs, chili, onion, vinegar, bacon, shrimp, and smoked fish.

12 ways of preparing avocado

RAW

With olive oil and vinegar or lemon
Pour olive oil and balsamic vinegar or lemon juice into the hollow left by the stone. Season with salt and pepper.

With mango, tomato, red onion, chili, cilantro, and lime
In a bowl, combine diced avocado, mango, and tomatoes. Combine with finely chopped red onion, chili, and cilantro. Add lime juice, olive oil, salt, and pepper and combine.

With tomato, cucumber, lemon, shallot, garlic, and ginger
In a bowl, combine diced avocado, tomato, and cucumber. Whisk together 1 part lemon juice, 2 parts olive oil, finely chopped shallot, crushed garlic, finely grated ginger, salt, and pepper. Toss the salad with the vinaigrette.

With edamame, soy, and rice vinegar
In a bowl, combine diced avocado with edamame beans. Whisk together 1 part light soy sauce, 1 part rice vinegar, 2 parts olive oil, salt, and pepper. Add the dressing to the avocado and edamame.

With potato, watercress, and lemon
In a bowl, combine chopped avocado, sliced, boiled new potatoes, and a handful of watercress. Season with olive oil, lemon juice, salt, and pepper. Goes well with smoked fish.

With beans or lentils, leek, tomato, and vinaigrette
In a bowl, combine chopped avocado, cooked beans or lentils, sliced leek, and halved cherry tomatoes. Whisk together 1 part vinegar with 3 parts oil, salt, and pepper. Add the vinaigrette to the bowl to coat the other ingredients.

With peanut butter, bread, lettuce, bacon, and lemon
Spread peanut butter on a slice of bread. Add a lettuce leaf, thinly sliced avocado, and crispy fried bacon. Season with pepper and drizzle with lemon juice.

With apple, celery, shallot, and vinegar
In a bowl, mash avocado and combine with finely cubed apple, celery, and shallot. Season with a dash of vinegar, salt, and pepper. Goes well with cooked chicken.

With cream cheese, lemon, and basil
In a bowl, mash avocado and combine with cream cheese. Toss with lemon juice, shredded basil, olive oil, salt, and pepper. Goes well on a slice of sourdough bread.

With white beans, garlic, chili, and lime
In a bowl, combine equal parts chopped avocado and drained, cooked white beans. Flavor with finely chopped garlic and chili, a dash of lime juice, olive oil, salt, and pepper. Tasty as a dip.

FRY

With egg, tomato, scallion, and baby leaf spinach
In a bowl, whisk together eggs with a little water, salt, and pepper. Heat olive oil in a skillet, pour in the egg mixture, and using a turner, pull the eggs toward the center. Repeat several times. Lower the heat and cook until the eggs have almost set. Add sliced avocado, tomato, scallion, and baby leaf spinach. Drizzle with olive oil and vinegar. Fold over and serve.

With leek and vinegar
Slice unripe avocado. Heat olive oil in a saucepan and add sliced leek. Add the avocado and season with vinegar, salt, and pepper. Goes well with gravlax or smoked salmon.

Avocado with egg, tomato, scallion, and baby leaf spinach. >

CUCUMBER

Cucumbers are clean, crisp, fresh, juicy, and versatile vegetables, almost synonymous with salads.

The long, crispy variety with dark green skin is the most popular cucumber, and is grown in greenhouses in colder climates as it needs warmth and a high level of nutrients. However, there are also more hardy varieties, which can be grown outdoors.

A cucumber contains as much as 96 percent water, and most of this is held around the core where the seeds lie. This is why some recipes recommend seeding the cucumber so there is less watery juice.

The best way to deseed a cucumber is to cut it in half lengthwise and scrape out the seeds with a teaspoon.

Cucumber is often eaten raw in cubes or slices, and can easily be grated. A favorite way to eat it in some countries is to steep thin slices in a bowl with a little vinegar, sugar, and dill, as an accompaniment to meat or fish.

Cucumbers can also be lightly fried, roasted, or added to a stir-fry. Cut into thick chunks to help preserve its shape in the high heat.

Gherkin is a variety of cucumber. It is shorter, fatter, and mostly used for pickling in either vinegar or salted water. It has a tougher skin, yet it is also good to eat raw.

STORING
Cucumber contains plenty of water and so does not survive well in extreme heat or cold. Store it in the vegetable drawer of the fridge, wrapped in a towel. Cucumber is not suitable for freezing.

SEASON
Cucumber is planted out several weeks after the last spring frost and can be harvested into the fall, all the way to the first hard frost.

GOES WELL WITH
Cucumber goes well with, for example, tomatoes, avocado, spinach, watermelon, chili, garlic, horseradish, ginger, herbs, olive, feta cheese, goat cheese, and yogurt.

< Cucumber with capers, scallion, and lemon.

19 ways of preparing cucumber

RAW
With sugar, vinegar, and dill or parsley
Peel and thinly slice cucumber. Place on a platter. Sprinkle with a little sugar, drizzle with vinegar, and set aside overnight in a cool place, until the sugar has dissolved. Season with salt and pepper and top with chopped dill or parsley.

With ginger, chili, soy, sugar, and sesame
Peel and thinly slice cucumber. Place in a bowl and combine with grated ginger and chopped chili. Season with light soy sauce and a pinch of sugar. Scatter over roasted sesame seeds.

With vinaigrette, honey, and dill
Peel and thinly slice cucumber. Place in a bowl. Whisk together 1 part white wine vinegar, 3 parts oil, honey, salt, and pepper. Add the vinaigrette and plenty of finely chopped dill to the bowl. Goes well with smoked salmon or spiced gravlax.

With yogurt, olive oil, lemon, mint, and olive
Flavor thick yogurt with a dash of olive oil, lemon juice, and chopped mint. Spread on a platter and scatter with sliced olives. Add diced cucumber. Season with salt, pepper, and drizzle with olive oil. Stir to combine.

With watermelon, ice cream, lemon, mint, and soda
Blend peeled and diced cucumber, chunks of watermelon, and a little water. Pour into a jug with plenty of ice, sliced lemon, and shredded mint. Top with a fruit soda such as lemon.

With watermelon, lemon dressing, feta cheese, olive, and basil
Peel cucumber, halve lengthwise, and scrape out the seeds with a spoon. Cube equal parts cucumber and watermelon. Put in a bowl. Whisk together 1 part lemon juice, 2 parts olive oil, salt, and pepper. Fold in the dressing. Crumble over feta cheese and top with black olives and shredded basil.

With crème fraîche, horseradish, and mustard
Peel cucumber, halve lengthwise, and scrape out the seeds with a spoon. Cube and place in a bowl with crème fraîche. Season with grated horseradish, Dijon mustard, salt, and pepper. Goes well with, for example, fried fish.

With fish roe, chive, and olive oil
Peel cucumber, halve lengthwise, and scrape out the seeds with a spoon. Cube and place in a bowl. Stir in fish roe, finely chopped chives, and a dash of olive oil. Season with salt and pepper. Goes well with, for example, bread and fish or cauliflower soup.

With garlic and yogurt
Peel cucumber, halve lengthwise, and scrape out the seeds with a spoon. Coarsely grate, then squeeze out the liquid and combine with grated garlic in a bowl. Coat with thick yogurt and olive oil. Season with salt and pepper.

With bell pepper, onion, green chili, lime, and olive oil
Peel cucumber, halve lengthwise, scrape out the seeds with a spoon and chop the cucumber. In a bowl, combine with diced bell peppers, sliced silver onions, and finely chopped green chili. Whisk together 1 part lime juice, 2 parts oil, and salt, add to the bowl, and stir to combine. Makes a good topping for tortillas.

With tomato, bell pepper, celery, onion, red chili, tomato juice, and garlic
Purée equal parts peeled and chopped cucumber, tomato, bell pepper, sliced celery, chopped onion, and red chili until smooth. Dilute with tomato juice to a soup consistency. Season with olive oil, crushed garlic, salt, and pepper. Serve chilled.

PICKLE
With vinegar, sugar, and dill

In a saucepan, cook 1 part vinegar, 2 parts powdered sugar, and 3 parts water. Let cool completely. Peel cucumber, halve lengthwise, scrape out the seeds with a spoon, and cut the flesh into cubes. Put in a jar with a lid with a couple of dill stems. Cover with the liquid, put on the lid, and stand for at least a couple of hours. Goes well with, for example, shrimp salad or breaded fish. Store in the fridge for about one week. The cucumber will lose its firmness the longer it remains in the vinegar.

FRY
With red onion, spinach, and vinegar

Peel cucumber, halve lengthwise, scrape out the seeds with a spoon, and slice the flesh. Fry in olive oil together with finely chopped red onion and shredded spinach over a low heat for a few minutes. Season with salt and pepper and drizzle with white wine vinegar.

With capers, scallion, and lemon

Peel cucumber, halve lengthwise, scrape out the seeds with a spoon, and slice the flesh. Fry in butter with capers and chopped scallions over a low heat for a few minutes. Season with salt, pepper, and lemon juice.

With onion, garlic, soy, chili, spinach, and sesame seeds

Peel cucumber, halve lengthwise, scrape out the seeds with a spoon, and thickly slice the flesh. Fry in oil with chopped onion and garlic on a low heat for a few minutes. Whisk together equal parts light soy sauce, olive oil, and chopped red chili. Stir into the skillet together with shredded spinach. Sprinkle with sesame seeds.

In the wok

Wok cooking is perfect for cucumber. Peel, halve and remove the seeds, then cut the cucumber flesh into thick slices before cooking over a high heat.

With leek, dill, and lemon

Peel cucumber, halve lengthwise, scrape out the seeds with a spoon, and cut the flesh into thick slices. Fry in butter together with sliced leek over a low heat for a few minutes. Season with chopped dill, lemon juice, salt, and pepper.

With radish, red onion, and chard or romaine lettuce

Peel cucumber, halve lengthwise, scrape out the seeds with a spoon, and cube the flesh. Fry in a skillet in oil and butter together with halved radishes over a low heat for a few minutes. Stir in thinly sliced red onion and shredded chard or romaine lettuce, and let them soften. Season with salt and pepper.

ROAST
With garlic, feta, and mint

Peel cucumber, halve lengthwise, scrape out the seeds with a spoon, and cut the flesh into thick slices. Place on a baking tray. Season with salt and pepper, add finely chopped garlic and drizzle with olive oil. Roast at 350 °F (175 °C) for about 10 minutes. Crumble over feta cheese and finely chopped mint.

PUMPKIN

Pumpkins are the best-known—and most delicious—of all winter squashes.

The flesh inside their hard yellow or orange skin is mild and fresh with undertones of honey. It varies in color from white to deep orange and is often quite stringy (this does not apply to butternut squash).

Pumpkins should be stored at room temperature where the skin hardens as they dry out. Thanks to their thick, hard skin, pumpkins can be stored over the winter. Some varieties (for example, red kuri squash), have relatively thin skins which don't need to be peeled, and this makes them less suitable for winter storage.

Cook pumpkin chunks until soft in salted water or stock, and combine with butter to make a purée; roasted and puréed pumpkin chunks give creamy soups extra character. It will acquire extra flavor if cooked with wine, chili, or ginger. Crumbled feta or goat cheese also work very well with pumpkin.

You can stir-fry thinly sliced or diced raw pumpkin. It is also very tasty cubed, coated with oil, and seasoned with garlic, thyme, salt, and pepper and baked in the oven until soft and golden brown.

STORING
Store pumpkin in a cool, dry place or in the vegetable drawer of the fridge. Once cut into pieces, pumpkin should be stored in the fridge. Puréed, parboiled, or cooked pumpkin is fine to freeze.

SEASON
Pumpkin is a long-growing crop that is started in late spring or early summer and harvested in fall before the first frost.

GOES WELL WITH
Pumpkin goes well with, for example, root vegetables, collard greens, garlic, chili, ginger, pine nuts, walnuts, hazelnuts, cumin, rosemary, cinnamon, butter, feta cheese, goat cheese, fish, chicken, pork, and game.

< Pumpkin with yellow onion, garlic, and herbs.

> **PEELING A PUMPKIN**
> Take care not to cut yourself when peeling a pumpkin. Start by halving it. Then, place the cut surface onto a cutting board, hold the pumpkin with one hand, and cut off the skin around the sides from the top down. Spoon out the seeds and cut the pumpkin flesh into wedges before processing further.

18 ways of preparing pumpkin

BOIL
With potato, cream, milk, thyme, garlic, and butter

Cut and cube 1 part pumpkin to 2 parts potatoes. Cook in a saucepan of salted water until soft. Drain and place in a bowl. In a saucepan, bring a mixture of equal parts cream and milk to the boil with thyme and crushed garlic. Strain. Mash the potato and pumpkin with a potato masher, add a pat of butter and dilute with the cream mixture until you have a smooth purée. Goes well with, for example, chicken.

With yellow onion, garlic, chili, white wine, stock, crème fraîche, ginger, and vinegar

Peel and cube the pumpkin. Fry in a skillet with oil, chopped yellow onion, garlic, and red chili for a few minutes. Add a dash of white wine, cover with vegetable stock, and simmer gently until soft. Blend until smooth with a spoonful of crème fraîche. Dilute with more stock until you have a smooth soup. Flavor with finely grated ginger, a dash of white wine vinegar, salt, and pepper. Serve with a dollop of cream cheese.

In soups and stews
Peel and cube the pumpkin, then simmer with other vegetables in soups and stews.

PICKLE
With vinegar, sugar, lemon, black pepper, and thyme

Peel and thinly slice pumpkin, then put the slices in a jar with a lid. In a saucepan, bring 1 part vinegar, 2 parts white sugar, 3 parts water, grated lemon zest, a couple of whole black peppercorns, and some thyme to the boil. Let cool a little. Cover the pumpkin with the warm liquid, put on the lid, and set aside for at least one day. Goes well with sandwiches. Store in the fridge for up to three months.

FRY
With egg and flour

In a bowl, whisk 1 egg and 1 tablespoon all-purpose flour per ½ cup (120 ml) pumpkin purée. Form into cakes and fry in a skillet. Goes well with sour cream, crumbled goat cheese, roasted pumpkin seeds, or crispy fried pork.

With garlic, rosemary, goat cheese, and pumpkin seeds

Peel and thinly slice pumpkin. In a bowl, combine the slices with olive oil, finely chopped garlic, chopped rosemary, salt, and pepper. Fry in a skillet for 4–5 minutes, or until soft and golden brown. Scatter with crumbled goat cheese and roasted pumpkin seeds.

With thyme, lemon, and garlic

Peel pumpkin and cut it into small cubes, then fry in a skillet with olive oil until soft. Add thyme, grated lemon zest, and finely chopped garlic, and fry for a few more minutes. Season with salt and pepper.

ROAST
With garlic, thyme, cream, and vinegar

Peel and chop pumpkin and place the pieces on a baking tray with oil, finely chopped garlic, thyme, salt, and pepper. Roast at 440 °F (220 °C) for about 15 minutes, or until golden brown. Heat a splash of cream in a saucepan. Add the pumpkin and combine with the cream to make a purée. Season with salt, pepper, and a dash of white wine vinegar. Goes well with, for example, roasted Brussels sprouts and chicken.

With garlic and vegetables
Peel and cut pumpkin into small chunks and place in an ovenproof dish with olive oil, salt, pepper, and halved garlic cloves. Roast at 440 °F (220 °C) for about 15 minutes, or until soft and golden brown. Other vegetables, such as carrots, parsnips, bell peppers, and celery root, can be roasted with the pumpkin.

With feta, pine nuts, and arugula
Serve oven-roasted pumpkin chunks with crumbled feta cheese and dry-roasted pine nuts, and stir together with some arugula.

With cream cheese, lemon, and basil
Season cream cheese with grated lemon zest, lemon juice, shredded basil, salt, and pepper. Serve with oven-roasted pumpkin.

With crème fraîche, garlic, chili, ginger, cilantro, and vinegar
Combine oven-roasted pumpkin chunks with crème fraîche to make a purée. Flavor with crushed garlic, chili sauce, grated ginger, chopped cilantro, a splash of red wine vinegar, salt, and pepper. Goes well with nacho chips or a slice of bread.

With garlic, kale or black kale, and goat cheese
Peel pumpkin, cut into wedges, and place on a baking tray with olive oil, finely chopped garlic, salt, and pepper. Roast at 400 °F (200 °C) for 15–20 minutes, or until soft. Top with shredded kale or black kale and bake until crispy. Crumble goat cheese on top.

With yellow onion, garlic, and herbs
Halve pumpkin and scoop out the seeds. Fill one half with chopped yellow onion, garlic, and fresh herbs. Add olive oil, salt, and pepper. Place the other half on top and wrap in aluminum foil. Bake at 350 °F (175 °C) for about 1 hour, or until soft. Goes well with broiled meat or fish.

With garlic, chili, black beans, and baby leaf spinach
Peel and chop pumpkin, then combine with oil, crushed garlic, sliced red chili, and salt, and place on a baking tray. Bake at 400 °F (200 °C) for about 20 minutes, or until soft and golden brown. Stir in cooked black beans and shredded baby leaf spinach.

With butter, sugar, cinnamon, cardamom, clove, and almonds
Peel and cube pumpkin, then place on a baking tray. Dot with butter and sprinkle with raw cane sugar, ground cinnamon, cardamom, and cloves. Bake at 350 °F (180 °C) for 15–20 minutes, or until soft. Scatter with flaked almonds 5 minutes before the end of the cooking time. Serve warm with vanilla ice cream.

BAKE
In a cake
Replace half the grated carrot in a carrot cake with grated pumpkin.

BROIL
With flavored butter or mayonnaise
Coat pumpkin wedges in oil, salt, and pepper. Broil until soft. Serve with mayonnaise or flavored butter (see pages 177 and 179). Goes well with, for example, broiled steak or chicken.

ZUCCHINI

Zucchini are small, delicately flavored green or yellow oblong summer squash harvested early in the season and available throughout the summer. In Italian, "zucchini" means small pumpkin: they are generally under 14 ounces (500 g) in weight and around 8 inches (20 cm) in length. The smaller the size, the tastier the flesh. Because of their thin skins, zucchini are not suitable for storing and should be eaten shortly after harvesting.

Zucchini consist of almost as much water as cucumbers. To make them less watery and for a firmer consistency, quarter lengthwise and scoop out the seeds, or sprinkle the flesh with salt and let stand for at least 30 minutes, rinse, then pat dry. The salt seasons the flesh and draws out the water from the zucchini.

Because their flavor is quite neutral, zucchini can be combined with most other vegetables. Cut raw zucchini into thin slices or small cubes and serve in a salad with vinegar, thinly sliced onion, and herbs. Fry together with broccoli florets, onions, and garlic, then transfer to a saucepan, add stock, and simmer to make a soup.

Zucchini love high temperatures. Brown rough chunks of zucchini, eggplant, bell peppers, onion, and garlic in oil in a skillet over a high heat, then combine with tomatoes. Coarsely chopped zucchini and garlic combined with crème fraîche and grated Parmesan cheese make a quick and easy supper dish served with freshly cooked pasta.

Marinate zucchini wedges or slices in a mixture of olive oil, lemon juice, chopped garlic, chili, and herbs before broiling or frying. Roast wedges along with other vegetables and crumble over feta or other goat cheese. Zucchini flowers are very attractive and also edible. Just cook them in oil in the deep fryer, or toss them in olive oil and add to risottos. Alternatively, stuff then fry them.

STORING
Store zucchini in the vegetable drawer of the fridge, preferably wrapped in a kitchen towel. Cooked zucchini can be frozen.

SEASON
Organic zucchini are harvested from summer to early fall.

GOES WELL WITH
Zucchini go well with, for example, tomatoes, bell peppers, eggplants, lemon, mint, feta cheese, Parmesan cheese, and goat cheese.

Zucchini with onion, baby leaf spinach, vinaigrette, sesame seeds, mayonnaise, and sriracha. >

21 ways of preparing zucchini

RAW

With onion, baby leaf spinach, vinaigrette, sesame seeds, mayonnaise, and sriracha

Thinly slice zucchini. In a bowl, combine with sliced onion, and baby leaf spinach. Whisk together 1 part vinegar, 3 parts olive oil, salt, and pepper. Fold the vinaigrette into the bowl and scatter over sesame seeds. Season mayonnaise with sriracha and serve with the zucchini salad.

With olive, lettuce, lemon dressing, and hot sauce

Thinly slice zucchini. In a bowl, combine with black olives and shredded lettuce leaves. Whisk together 1 part lemon juice, 2 parts olive oil, grated lemon zest, hot sauce, and salt. Add the dressing to the bowl.

With onion, celery, lettuce, lemon dressing, and pumpkin seeds

Cut zucchini into very thin slices, preferably with a mandolin slicer. In a bowl, combine with thinly sliced onion, celery, and shredded lettuce leaves. Whisk together 1 part lemon juice, 2 parts olive oil, a little grated lemon zest, salt, and pepper. Add the dressing to the bowl, stir well to combine, and sprinkle with roasted pumpkin seeds.

With mint, feta, and vinaigrette

Thinly slice zucchini. In a bowl, combine with shredded mint, and crumbled feta cheese. Whisk together 1 part vinegar, 3 parts olive oil, salt, and pepper. Add the vinaigrette to the bowl and stir to combine.

With arugula, pesto, vinegar, and Parmesan

Very thinly slice zucchini. In a bowl, combine with arugula. Stir in pesto and a splash of red wine vinegar. Add grated Parmesan cheese and season with pepper.

With pasta, olive oil, Parmesan, and basil

Very thinly slice zucchini and add to freshly cooked pasta. Stir in olive oil, grated Parmesan, and fresh basil. Season with salt and pepper.

BOIL

With leek and carrot

Thinly slice zucchini, leek, and carrot and add to pasta in a saucepan for the last few minutes of the cooking time.

With onion, garlic, stock, cream, pesto, and Parmesan

Cut zucchini into cubes. Fry in a skillet with oil, chopped onion, and garlic for a few minutes without browning. Cover with vegetable stock, put on the lid, and simmer for about 10 minutes, or until the zucchini are soft. Blend with cream to make a soup. Dilute with more stock until it has the desired consistency. Flavor with pesto, salt, and pepper. Serve with grated Parmesan cheese and a few drops of olive oil.

FRY

With vinaigrette, Parmesan, shallot, and basil

Cut zucchini into finger-thick slices. Fry in olive oil until golden brown. Season with salt and pepper, and transfer to a bowl. Whisk together 1 part red wine vinegar, 3 parts olive oil, grated Parmesan cheese, finely chopped shallot, shredded basil, salt, and pepper. Add the vinaigrette to the bowl.

With onion, garlic, and ground beef

Coarsely chop zucchini and fry in olive oil with chopped onion and garlic until soft. Let cool and combine with ground beef for making burgers.

With garlic, lemon, parsley, pasta, and Parmesan

Coarsely grate the zucchini. Fry in olive oil with chopped garlic until soft and golden brown. Season with lemon juice, chopped parsley, salt, and pepper. Stir into freshly cooked pasta and serve with grated Parmesan cheese.

With mushrooms, red onion, and garlic

Cut zucchini into cubes and mushrooms into wedges. Fry both in olive oil, together with sliced red onion and finely chopped garlic until soft and golden brown. Season with salt and pepper, and add to risotto, pasta, rice, couscous, or other grains.

With flour, egg, polenta, and Parmesan

Cut zucchini into finger-thick slices. In a bowl, combine with a batter made from all-purpose flour, whisked eggs, and polenta. Fry in olive oil until golden brown. Drain on paper towels. Season with salt and pepper, and grate over Parmesan cheese.

With eggplant, bell pepper, yellow onion, garlic, tomato, and basil

Fry equal-sized chunks of zucchini, eggplant, and bell peppers in oil with chopped onion and garlic. Place in a saucepan and add cubed or canned tomatoes. Season with salt and pepper, put on the lid, and simmer for about 1 hour, or until the vegetables are soft. Sprinkle with basil before serving.

With leek, garlic, egg, and feta

Thinly slice zucchini. Fry in oil together with sliced leek and garlic until soft and golden brown. Season with salt and pepper. In a bowl, whisk together eggs, a dash of water, salt, and pepper. Pour the batter over the zucchini and using a turner, pull the eggs from the edges to the center. Repeat several times. Reduce the heat and fry the omelet until the eggs are almost completely set. Top with crumbled feta cheese and fold over.

With garlic, crème fraîche, pasta, and Parmesan

Coarsely grate zucchini and fry in butter together with finely chopped garlic until soft and golden brown. Add crème fraîche and stir together to make a sauce. Season with salt and pepper. Fold the sauce into freshly cooked pasta and top with grated Parmesan cheese.

With vinegar, soy, sesame, and garlic

Cut zucchini into finger-thick slices and fry in oil until golden brown. In a bowl, whisk together 1 part white wine vinegar, 1 part oil, 2 parts light soy sauce, a dash of sesame oil, and some crushed garlic. Stir the vinaigrette into the zucchini. Season with salt and pepper, and add sesame seeds. Goes well with, for example, fried tofu.

ROAST
With tomato and garlic

Cut zucchini into cubes and halve cherry tomatoes. Place both on a baking tray with olive oil, grated garlic, salt, and pepper. Roast at 440 °F (220 °C) for about 15 minutes, or until the vegetables have turned golden brown. Combine with pasta, couscous, or other grains.

With tomato, herbs, and Parmesan

Cut zucchini and tomatoes into thin slices, then place in an ovenproof dish. Add olive oil, salt, pepper, and chopped fresh herbs, such as basil or marjoram, and grated Parmesan cheese. Bake at 440 °F (220 °C) for about 15 minutes, or until the cheese is golden.

With garlic and rosemary

Cut zucchini into cubes and place on a baking tray with olive oil, grated garlic, chopped rosemary, salt, and pepper. Roast at 440 °F (220 °C) for about 15–20 minutes, or until golden brown.

BROIL
With halloumi, vinaigrette, tomato, and shallot

Slice zucchini and halloumi and brush with olive oil. Broil until golden brown. Place on a platter. Whisk together 1 part vinegar, 3 parts olive oil, finely chopped tomatoes, finely chopped shallot, salt, and pepper. Pour the vinaigrette over the zucchini and halloumi slices.

EGGPLANT

Eggplant are prized for their beautiful purple skin, taste, and texture. They have been bred to be less bitter over the last twenty years or so but have retained their unique flavor. You can lessen any remaining bitterness and prepare eggplant for frying by salting individual slices and letting them sit for at least 20 minutes to "sweat." Wipe each slice clean with a paper towel. Salting may create a firmer texture because the eggplant won't absorb the same amount of fat or liquid during cooking.

As the eggplant is quite delicate, fry chopped or sliced eggplant at a high temperature to prevent the flesh from falling apart when they are to be cooked in sauces or in a dish such as ratatouille.

It is perfectly acceptable to retain the eggplant skin as it can hold the slices or cubes together during cooking. If you want to make an eggplant purée, you can easily scrape the flesh from the skin once it is cooked. Only the skin of very young eggplants can be eaten.

STORING
Eggplant is cold sensitive. Store in a kitchen towel in the vegetable drawer of the fridge. You can freeze cooked eggplant.

SEASON
Organic eggplant is harvested from high summer to early fall. However, because eggplant is heat loving, it is often imported from warmer zones.

GOES WELL WITH
Eggplant goes well with Parmesan cheese, zucchini, bell pepper, tomatoes, cauliflower, chard, herbs, onion, garlic, pasta, lamb, chicken, fish, and broiled dishes.

< Eggplant with thyme, garlic, goat cheese, and lemon.

20 ways of preparing eggplant

FRY
With garlic and white beans
Cut eggplant in cubes and fry in olive oil until golden brown. Top with chopped garlic, salt, and pepper. Add cooked white beans and serve with a green salad.

With zucchini, garlic, sausage, scallion, herbs, pita, and sour cream
Cut eggplant and zucchini in cubes. Fry in olive oil with chopped garlic until soft, then add sliced sausage and fry for a couple more minutes. Add sliced scallion and chopped herbs. Season with salt and pepper. Scoop into pita bread pockets and serve with sour cream.

With garlic, chili, rosemary, thyme, tomato, and vinaigrette
Cut eggplant into cubes and fry in olive oil together with sliced garlic, chopped red chili, chopped rosemary, and thyme until golden brown. Season with salt. Arrange sliced tomatoes on a plate. Whisk together 1 part white wine vinegar, 3 parts olive oil, salt, and pepper. Spread the vinaigrette over the tomatoes and cover with the eggplant mixture.

With zucchini, garlic, tomato sauce, and Parmesan
Cut eggplant and zucchini in cubes, and fry in olive oil together with sliced garlic, salt, and pepper until golden brown. Stir in tomato sauce and serve over freshly cooked pasta with grated Parmesan cheese.

With bell pepper, onion, garlic, herbs, and chili
Cut eggplant and zucchini in cubes. Combine with finely chopped onion and garlic, and sauté in olive oil until golden brown. Flavor with finely chopped herbs of your choice, salt, and chili. Combine with grated cauliflower, couscous, or rice.

With mint, garlic, and pine nuts
Thinly slice and fry eggplant in olive oil until soft and golden brown. In a bowl, combine olive oil, chopped mint, and crushed garlic. Dry-roast pine nuts in a hot skillet. Season with salt and pepper. Scatter the mint mixture and pine nuts over the eggplant slices.

In lasagna
Replace a layer of pasta sheets with fried eggplant slices when preparing a lasagna.

With thyme, garlic, goat cheese, rocket, and lemon
Cut the eggplant into wedges and fry in olive oil over a medium heat until soft. Increase the heat to high and brown the eggplant. Add chopped fresh thyme and chopped garlic, and cook for a few more minutes. Season with salt and pepper. Transfer to a plate and top with crumbled goat cheese, rocket and lemon juice.

DEEP-FRY
With egg, Parmesan, flour, and panko breadcrumbs
Whisk together eggs, grated Parmesan cheese, salt, and pepper. Thinly slice eggplant and coat first with all-purpose flour, then the egg mix, and lastly with panko breadcrumbs. Deep-fry the slices in a generous amount of olive oil until golden brown. Drain on paper towels. Serve hot or cold, as a snack, side dish, or as a main course with a side salad.

ROAST
With cauliflower, garlic, chili, and thyme
Thickly slice eggplant and cauliflower and place in an ovenproof dish with olive oil, chopped garlic, chili, and fresh or dried thyme. Season with salt and pepper. Roast at 400 °F (200 °C) for 20–30 minutes, or until soft and golden brown.

With garlic, ground beef, and Parmesan
Halve an eggplant, cover the cut surfaces with olive oil and chopped garlic, and season with salt and pepper. Roast at 400 °F (200 °C) for about 15–20 minutes, or until soft and golden brown. Fill the sunken cut surfaces

with browned ground beef and grated Parmesan cheese. Return to the oven and roast at 430°F (220°C) until the cheese begins to brown.

With tomato sauce, basil, Parmesan, and butter

Thinly slice eggplant and fry in a skillet with olive oil. Season with salt and pepper and cook until golden brown. Drain on paper towels. Layer the slices in an ovenproof dish and top with tomato sauce, shredded basil, and grated Parmesan cheese. Top each slice with a pat of butter and roast at 400°F (200°C) for about 30 minutes, or until the cheese has melted and browned.

With potato, garlic, chili, and thyme

Thickly slice eggplant and potato and toss in olive oil with chopped garlic, chili, and thyme. Season with salt and pepper. Roast at 400°F (200°C) for 20–30 minutes, or until soft and golden brown. Goes well with chicken.

With garlic, chili, halloumi, basil, and lemon

Cut eggplant into wedges and arrange on a baking tray. Whisk together chopped garlic, finely chopped chili, and olive oil. Pour the mixture over the wedges, and season with salt and pepper. Roast at 400°F (200°C) for about 15 minutes, or until soft and golden brown. Sprinkle with grated halloumi cheese and return to the oven for two minutes, or until the cheese is just melting. Sprinkle with shredded basil and drizzle with lemon juice.

With garlic and sumac

Cut eggplant into wedges and arrange on a baking tray. Whisk together olive oil, chopped garlic, and sumac. Rub the mixture onto the eggplant and season with salt and pepper. Bake at 400°F (200°C) for about 15 minutes, or until soft and golden brown.

With mayonnaise, garlic, and lemon

Cut eggplant into wedges. Toss in olive oil and arrange on a baking tray. Season with salt and pepper, and roast at 400°F (200°C) for about 15 minutes, or until soft and golden brown. Let cool, and remove and discard the eggplant skins. Combine the flesh with an equal amount of mayonnaise. Flavor with finely chopped garlic, lemon juice, salt, and pepper. Goes well with broiled dishes.

With chili, butter, herbs, and vinegar

Cut eggplant into wedges. Toss in olive oil and arrange on a baking tray. Season with salt and pepper and roast at 400°F (200°C) for about 15 minutes, or until soft and golden brown. Combine 1 part chili sauce, 1 part butter, and chopped herbs in a saucepan. Season with salt, pepper, and a dash of vinegar. Cook over a medium heat until just bubbling. Serve the sauce with the eggplant.

With garlic and lemon

Place whole eggplant onto a baking tray. Pierce the skin with a sharp knife and press coarsely chopped garlic into the cuts. Roast at 400°F (200°C) for about 20 minutes. Halve the eggplant, scrape out the flesh, and combine with olive oil, lemon juice, and salt. Goes well with broiled dishes.

BROIL

With zucchini, olive oil, vinaigrette, and basil

Thickly slice eggplant and zucchini. Brush with olive oil and broil on both sides. Transfer to a plate with whole olives. Whisk together 1 part balsamic vinegar, 3 parts olive oil, salt, and pepper to taste. Pour the vinaigrette over the slices and top with chopped basil. Goes well with broiled meat and rye bread.

With olive oil

Broil a whole eggplant slowly until it is completely soft—don't worry if it burns slightly. Make a deep cut in the eggplant to create a pocket. Drizzle olive oil into the pocket and return to the broiler for a couple more minutes. Scrape out the eggplant flesh and place in a bowl. Season with salt and more olive oil as desired. Goes well with broiled dishes.

BELL PEPPER

Green bell peppers are harvested before the fruit is fully ripe. They have a bitter, grassy taste and are mostly served raw in salads, but can be cooked in a stew or in a wok, which releases a milder flavor.

Ripe, red bell peppers are considerably sweeter and fruitier. The skin can be bitter, so if you are looking for maximum sweetness, peel before roasting or broiling. Skin bell peppers by laying them on a foil-lined broiler pan under a high heat and cooking until blackened. Let cool, then remove the skin. Peeled bell peppers can be used in many ways: shredded in salads, as a snack, or puréed for soups. Keep the skin on when cooking bell peppers in a sauce or pan-frying them.

Bell peppers can also be broiled. Place a couple of bell peppers under the broiler, or directly on the barbecue. When browned, let cool, halve, and remove the seeds. Bell peppers can then be placed in a jar, covered with olive oil, and stored in the fridge for up to two weeks. Alternatively, you can thread uncooked slices of bell pepper onto a skewer together with fish, meat, or other vegetables and broil or barbecue them.

Ramiro is an oblong, tapered pepper with red, yellow, and green variations. It is sweeter than regular bell peppers but is used in the same way. Roast peeled bell peppers with butter, olive oil, garlic, and anchovies.

STORING
Store bell peppers wrapped in a kitchen towel in the fridge. Cooked bell peppers can be frozen.

SEASON
Bell peppers require a long growing season and are usually started in spring before the last frost. They thrive in hot summers, and are grown year-round as a greenhouse plant.

GOES WELL WITH
Bell peppers go well with, for example, cornes, eggplant, zucchini, tomatoes, onion, garlic, and olives.

< Bell peppers with butter, olive oil, garlic, and anchovies.

19 ways of preparing bell pepper

RAW
With tomato, red onion, garlic, chili, lime, and cilantro
Seed and finely chop green bell pepper and tomato. In a bowl, combine with finely chopped red onion, garlic, and green chili. Flavor with olive oil, lime, chopped cilantro, and salt. Marinate for 30 minutes.

With avocado, red onion, garlic, kidney beans, vinaigrette, and basil
Chop red bell peppers. In a bowl, combine with cubed avocado, finely chopped red onion, crushed garlic, and cooked kidney beans. Whisk together 1 part red wine vinegar, 3 parts olive oil, chopped basil, salt, and pepper. Fold the vinaigrette into the salad. Goes well with chicken and spare ribs.

With onion, black beans, lemon dressing, herbs, and chili
Cut bell pepper into small cubes. In a bowl, combine with finely chopped onion and cooked black beans. Whisk together 1 part lemon juice and 2 parts olive oil. Add the dressing to the bowl with chopped herbs, such as oregano, parsley, and coriander, and season with chili powder and salt.

FRY
With shallot, garlic, tomato, and basil or oregano
Cut bell pepper into strips and combine with sliced shallot and garlic. Fry in oil for a few minutes without browning them. Add coarsely chopped tomato and simmer for 10 minutes. Flavor with shredded basil or oregano, salt, and pepper. Goes well with, fish.

With chili, garlic, and sourdough bread
Chop bell peppers. Fry in olive oil together with chopped red chili and crushed garlic for a couple of minutes. Tear in chunks of day-old sourdough bread and fry together. Season with salt and pepper. Works well as a spicy addition to a chili con carne.

With zucchini, red onion, garlic, olive, feta, and basil
Cut bell peppers and zucchini into cubes. Fry in olive oil together with chopped red onion and crushed garlic for a few minutes. Season with salt and pepper and arrange on a platter. Top with black olives, crumbled feta cheese, and chopped basil. Goes well with pasta.

With zucchini, yellow onion, garlic, egg, Parmesan, and chive
Cut bell pepper into strips. Fry in olive oil for a few minutes with chopped zucchini, sliced yellow onion, and garlic. Season with salt and pepper. In a bowl, whisk together eggs, grated Parmesan cheese, finely chopped chives, salt, and pepper. Pour the mixture over the vegetables and, using a turner, pull from the edges to the center. Repeat several times. Lower the heat and cook the omelet until set.

ROAST
Roasted whole
Place whole bell peppers on a greased baking tray. Roast at 400 °F (200 °C) for 15 minutes, or until the skin has blistered. Place the hot bell peppers in a bowl, cover with plastic wrap, and let cool. Peel the bell peppers, halve, and remove the seeds. Use the bell peppers straightaway, or pour the liquid from the bowl into a glass jar, add the peppers, and cover with olive oil. Can be stored in the fridge for a up to two weeks.

With olive, red onion, and vinaigrette

In a bowl, combine oven-roasted, peeled bell peppers, olives, and thinly sliced red onion. Whisk together 1 part red wine vinegar, 3 parts olive oil, salt, and pepper. Add the vinaigrette to the bowl and stir to combine.

With ricotta and basil

In a bowl, combine slices of oven-roasted, peeled bell pepper, ricotta cheese, and shredded basil. Season with salt and pepper. Goes well with air-dried ham as a side dish.

With pasta

Gently heat oven-roasted, peeled bell peppers in a saucepan with olive oil and season with salt and pepper. Fold the sauce into freshly cooked pasta.

With butter, olive oil, garlic, and anchovies

Placed oven-roasted, peeled bell peppers in a bowl. Heat equal parts butter and olive oil in a saucepan over a low heat. Add thinly sliced garlic and coarsely chopped anchovies and simmer for about 5 minutes, or until the garlic is soft, but not browned. Pour the mixture over the bell peppers and serve. Goes well with broiled fish and meat.

With crème fraîche, garlic, vinegar, and herbs

Blend oven-roasted, peeled, and chopped bell peppers with a spoonful of crème fraîche. Combine and season with finely chopped garlic, a dash of red wine vinegar, chopped herbs, salt, and pepper. Goes well with, for example, broiled chicken.

With tomato, garlic, and almonds

Blend oven-roasted, peeled, and chopped bell peppers, chopped tomato, garlic, blanched almonds, and olive oil to make a smooth sauce. Season with salt and pepper. Goes well with broiled chicken.

With zucchini, potato, onion, garlic, and rosemary

Coarsely chop bell peppers, zucchini, and potatoes and place on a baking tray or in an ovenproof dish with onion wedges. In a bowl, combine finely chopped garlic, coarsely chopped rosemary, and olive oil. Spread over the vegetables. Season with salt and pepper. Roast at 400 °F (200 °C) for about 20 minutes, or until the vegetables are golden brown.

With potato, onion, Manchego, egg, and milk or cream

Cut bell peppers into cubes, and place in an ovenproof dish with sliced cooked potato and onion. Whisk together milk or cream (1 egg per ½ cup/120 ml) and pour over the vegetables. Sprinkle with grated Manchego cheese. Season with salt and pepper and roast at 350 °F (170 °C) for 20 minutes, or until the egg mixture has set. Goes well with, for example, fried chorizo.

BROIL
Broil and peel

Coat whole bell peppers in oil and place under the broiler for 15 minutes, or until the skins have blistered. Transfer the bell peppers to a bowl, cover with plastic wrap, and let cool. Peel the bell peppers, halve, and remove the seeds. Use the bell peppers straightaway, or pour the liquid from the bowl into a glass jar, add the peppers and cover with olive oil. Can be stored in the fridge for up to two weeks.

With tapenade and Manchego

Halve Ramiro or regular bell peppers and remove the seeds and membranes. Brush with oil and broil until soft and golden brown. Add a few spoonfuls of tapenade and grated Manchego cheese.

With goat cheese, eggplant purée, or Parmesan mayonnaise

Serve broiled bell peppers with eggplant and olive oil purée (see page 167) or Parmesan mayonnaise (see page 177).

TOMATO

Tomatoes are one of the most widely grown crops on the planet, with almost 1,000 varieties of different shapes and colors, including yellow, red, orange, green, and purple. After a long period of focusing on appearance and shelf life, tomato growers have now turned their attention to taste. So far, however, it has been difficult for store-bought tomatoes to come anywhere near the flavor of locally grown, farmers' market tomatoes, which are harvested fully ripened and transported a short distance only.

Raw tomatoes are perfect served simply with sliced red onion, torn basil leaves, olive oil, salt, and pepper. Enjoy as a side dish with pasta, on bruschetta, or as a deliciously fresh, summery tomato salad.

For cooking, it is usually recommended to peel tomatoes, as the chunky pieces of skin can be unpleasant in smooth sauces and purées. Peel tomatoes by cutting a cross in the top of each one and placing them in a bowl of boiling water for about 10 seconds. Lift out with tongs, cool in iced water, and remove the skin. It should come off easily. However, if the tomatoes are cooked in a sauce or in a soup, it is often recommended you pass the cooked tomatoes through a strainer, which will remove the tomato skin.

Tomatoes will have a more pronounced flavor if you either cook them in a saucepan, or roast on a low heat in the oven.

If you have a glut of tomatoes, you can freeze them whole with or without the skin. Another tip is to have a few batches of ready-made tomato sauce in the freezer, which is easy to serve with pasta or dilute with stock to make a soup. Preserved and pickled tomatoes, tomato purée, or tomato ketchup are other delicious ways of using up a large crop of tomatoes.

STORING
Tomatoes are cold sensitive and are best kept at room temperature. If they are stored in a cold environment, then the sugar content will decrease, and the maturation process will be halted. It is perfectly fine to freeze tomatoes with or without the skin.

SEASON
Organically grown tomatoes cultivated in heated greenhouses can be harvested from spring to late fall, and in unheated greenhouses from early summer to early fall.

GOES WELL WITH
Tomatoes go well with, for example, bell pepper, eggplant, avocado, herbs, onion, garlic, chili, capers, olives, olive oil, vinegar, mozzarella cheese, Parmesan cheese, feta cheese, anchovies, and bacon.

Tomatoes with onion, olive oil, vinegar, and dill. >

20 ways of preparing tomato

RAW

With shallot, anchovies, olive oil, vinegar, and parsley

Slice tomatoes. Place them on a platter and scatter with thinly sliced shallot and anchovies. Drizzle with olive oil and red wine vinegar. Season with salt and pepper and sprinkle with chopped parsley.

With onion, olive oil, vinegar, and dill

Slice tomatoes and onions and place them on a platter. Drizzle with olive oil and a few drops of red wine vinegar. Season with salt and pepper and sprinkle with chopped dill.

With scallion, egg, dill, lemon, and butter

Thinly slice tomatoes and place in a bowl with sliced scallions. Peel and halve hard-boiled eggs and add to the bowl with chopped dill and lemon juice. Season with salt and pepper and drizzle with melted butter. Goes well with, for example, baked salmon.

With lemon dressing, cucumber, red onion, feta, and basil

Slice tomatoes and place on a platter. In a bowl, combine 1 part lemon juice, 2 parts olive oil, diced cucumber, thinly sliced red onion, crumbled feta cheese, chopped basil, salt, and pepper. Pour over the tomatoes.

With sun-dried tomato, black olive, shallot, basil, and vinaigrette

Place sliced tomatoes on a platter. In a bowl, combine shredded sun-dried tomatoes, sliced black olives, finely chopped shallots, and torn basil. Whisk together 1 part balsamic vinegar, 3 parts olive oil, salt, and pepper. Pour over the tomatoes. Goes well with beef carpaccio.

PICKLE

With vinegar, sugar, black pepper, and herbs

Peel cherry tomatoes and place in a jar with a lid. In a saucepan, heat 1 part vinegar, 2 parts powdered sugar, 3 parts water, and black peppercorns. Cover the tomatoes with the warm liquid, put on the lid securely, and set aside to marinate for at least one day. Remove the tomatoes. Place them in a serving bowl and add some chopped herbs (for example, dill is recommended, if the tomatoes are to be served with fish, and basil, if served with chicken). Store in the fridge for up to 3 months.

BOIL

Quick tomato sauce

Chop tomatoes and fry in a saucepan with olive oil, chopped yellow onion, and garlic. Cover with a lid and simmer for about 10 minutes. Season with salt and pepper. Enjoy with freshly cooked pasta.

Tomato sauce or tomato soup

Fry equal amounts of chopped yellow onion, carrot, and celery with chopped garlic until soft. Add chopped tomatoes, stir, and cover with a lid. Cook over a medium heat for 25 minutes, stirring occasionally. Add shredded parsley and basil and simmer for another 5 minutes, or until the sauce has the desired consistency. Season with salt and pepper. To make a soup, stir in stock and a splash of cream.

With yellow onion, cream, anchovies, cherry tomato, and dill

Fry chopped yellow onion in a skillet with butter until soft but without browning. Pour in cream and cook for 5–10 minutes, or until thickened. Season with chopped anchovies. Add halved cherry tomatoes and cook for a few more minutes. Garnish with chopped dill and season with salt and pepper. Goes well with fish.

With potato, stock, dill, and butter

Peel and chop potatoes. Cook in a saucepan with vegetable stock until tender. Add chopped tomatoes, chopped dill, and a pat of butter. Cook until the potatoes are soft. Season with salt and pepper. Serve with, for example, fish.

With lemon, ginger, and sugar

Combine lemon juice, grated lemon zest, and grated ginger in a saucepan. Scatter over some powdered sugar. Add halved cherry tomatoes and simmer for about 20 minutes, or until the mixture is the consistency of jam. Goes well with cheese.

FRY
With onion, egg, cheese, cherry tomato, and basil

Fry sliced onion in olive oil until soft. In a bowl, whisk together eggs, a splash of water, salt, and pepper. Pour the mixture over the onion and pull it from the edges toward the center with a turner. Repeat several times. Reduce the heat and fry the omelet until the eggs are almost set. Add sliced tomatoes or halved cherry tomatoes and grated hard cheese. Season with salt and pepper and garnish with shredded basil.

With cornmeal, mozzarella cheese, and basil

Coat thick slices of tomato with fine cornmeal. Fry in plenty of olive oil until golden brown. Season with salt and pepper. Drain on paper towels. Serve hot with sliced mozzarella cheese and shredded basil.

ROAST
Oven-dried

Place whole cherry tomatoes, olive oil, salt, and pepper on a baking tray. Roast at 200 °F (100 °C) for about 2 hours, or until soft. Serve with drinks or as a side dish with broiled meat, fried fish, or roasted chicken.

Sauce with garlic, herbs, and Parmesan

Cut tomatoes into rough chunks. Combine with sliced garlic and herbs on a baking tray. Drizzle with olive oil, salt, and pepper. Roast at 300 °F (150 °C) for about 45 minutes, or until soft. Blend if you want a smoother sauce. Serve with freshly cooked pasta and grated Parmesan cheese.

With garlic, lemon, thyme, and olive oil

Cut tomatoes in half and place on a baking tray, with the cut sides facing up. Combine garlic, grated lemon zest, fresh thyme, and olive oil. Sprinkle over the tomatoes. Season with salt and pepper. Roast at 400 °F (200 °C) for about 20 minutes. Goes well with broiled fish.

With fish fillet, thyme, and garlic

Cut white fish fillet into equal-sized portions. Arrange on an ovenproof dish with whole cherry tomatoes. Season with salt and pepper and scatter over fresh thyme and sliced garlic. Drizzle with olive oil and roast at 350 °F (175 °C) for about 15 minutes, or until the fish is cooked.

With bread, garlic, olive oil, and basil

Toast slices of bread. Rub one side of the warm toast with garlic and drizzle with olive oil. In a bowl, combine sliced tomatoes, olive oil, shredded basil, salt, and pepper. Spread on the slices of toast.

BROIL
With garlic

Halve tomatoes. Rub the cut surfaces with garlic and brush with olive oil. Season with salt and pepper and broil.

With fish, scallion, dill, and butter

Slice tomatoes and place on pieces of aluminum foil with fish fillets, sliced scallion, chopped dill, and a pat of butter. Close with the seam facing upward. Broil for about 15 minutes.

DIPS AND COLD SAUCES

MAYONNAISE

BASIC MAYONNAISE
2 egg yolks
1–2 tsp vinegar
1 tsp Dijon mustard
1¼ cups (300 ml) canola oil
Dash of water (optional)
Salt and pepper

In a bowl, beat together the egg yolks, vinegar, and mustard. Whisking constantly, add the oil, one drop at a time. Dilute with water if the mayonnaise is too thick. Season with salt and pepper.

Mayonnaise plus grated lemon zest, lemon juice or Dijon mustard, salt, and pepper.

Mayonnaise plus lemon juice, and finely grated Parmesan cheese.

Mayonnaise plus grated garlic, lemon juice, salt, and pepper.

Mayonnaise plus finely chopped capers, lemon juice, salt, and pepper.

Mayonnaise plus finely chopped basil, grated Parmesan cheese, crushed garlic, lemon juice, salt, and pepper.

Mayonnaise plus light soy sauce.

Mayonnaise plus light soy sauce and wasabi.

Mayonnaise plus light soy sauce, sesame oil, and roasted sesame seeds.

Mayonnaise, light soy sauce, hot sauce, and roasted sesame seeds.

Mayonnaise plus light soy sauce, and sriracha or roasted sesame seeds.

Mayonnaise plus light soy sauce or lemon juice, sriracha, crushed garlic, salt, and pepper.

Mayonnaise plus crème fraîche, tapenade, grated lemon zest, lemon juice, salt, and pepper.

Mayonnaise plus sour cream, finely chopped apple, curry, white wine vinegar, salt, and pepper.

Mayonnaise plus sour cream, grated Parmesan cheese, white wine vinegar, salt, and pepper.

Mayonnaise plus avocado, crushed garlic, lemon juice, salt, and pepper.

DIPS & COLD SAUCES

YOGURT

Thick yogurt plus honey, finely chopped ginger, chive, olive oil, salt, and pepper.

Thick yogurt plus avocado, finely chopped garlic, lime or lemon juice, chopped cilantro, salt, and pepper.

Thick yogurt plus olive oil, lemon juice, finely chopped mint, salt, and pepper.

Thick yogurt plus lemon juice, chili paste, and salt.

CREAM

Crème fraîche plus balsamic vinegar, salt, and pepper.

Crème fraîche plus crushed garlic, chili paste, a dash of red wine vinegar, salt, and pepper.

Sour cream plus apple vinegar, honey, applesauce, chive, salt and pepper.

Sour cream plus roe, lemon juice, chopped dill and pepper.

CHEESE

Gorgonzola plus heavy cream, white wine vinegar, and black pepper.

Blue cheese plus a few drops of water and flavored with vinegar, olive oil, and pepper.

Blue cheese plus crème fraîche, salt, and pepper.

Goat cheese plus crème fraîche and pepper.

Feta cheese plus crème fraîche, finely chopped red onion, coarsely ground black pepper, and olive oil.

Cream cheese plus parsley, and flavored with lemon juice, salt, and pepper.

Cream cheese plus mashed avocado, lemon juice, olive oil, shredded basil, salt, and pepper.

Cream cheese plus grated lemon zest, lemon juice, olive oil, finely chopped herbs of your choice, salt, and pepper.

Cream cheese plus grated fresh horseradish, salt, and pepper.

SOY SAUCE

Equal parts light soy sauce and sweet chili sauce, and perhaps some fish sauce.

Equal parts light soy sauce, orange juice, and olive oil, flavored with finely chopped ginger and pepper.

FLAVORED BUTTER

Butter plus lemon zest, lemon juice, salt, and pepper.

Butter plus finely chopped garlic, salt, and pepper.

Butter plus lemon juice, finely chopped garlic, finely chopped herbs of your choice, salt, and pepper.

Butter plus coarsely minced capers, lemon zest, chopped watercress, fresh lemon juice, salt, and pepper.

Butter plus finely chopped chilis, finely chopped mint, lemon juice, salt, and pepper.

Butter plus finely chopped anchovies and/or lemon juice, salt, and pepper.

Butter plus tapenade, and pepper.

Butter plus grated Parmesan cheese, salt, and pepper.

Butter plus finely chopped herbs of your choice, garlic, salt, and pepper.

Butter plus finely chopped chili, and salt.

Butter plus paprika, cayenne pepper, salt, and pepper.

Butter plus chili paste, and salt.

Butter plus deep-fried garlic (see page 132), salt, and pepper.

Browned butter plus finely chopped blanched almonds or hazelnuts, and parsley.

Browned butter plus capers, finely chopped dill, grated lemon zest, and lemon juice.

DIPS & COLD SAUCES

VINAIGRETTE

> **BASIC VINAIGRETTE**
> 1 part vinegar
> 3 parts oil
> Salt and pepper
>
> Whisk vinegar and oil together in a bowl. Season with salt and pepper.

> **BASIC LEMON DRESSING**
> 1 part fresh lemon juice
> 2 parts oil
> Salt and pepper
>
> Whisk lemon juice and oil together in a bowl. Season with salt and pepper.

Basic vinaigrette plus Dijon mustard.

Basic vinaigrette plus honey.

Basic vinaigrette plus finely chopped scallion.

Basic vinaigrette plus finely chopped scallion, and finely chopped olives.

Basic vinaigrette plus finely chopped scallion, and finely chopped tomatoes.

Basic vinaigrette plus diced apples, salt, and pepper.

Basic lemon dressing plus grated lemon zest, grated ginger, salt, and pepper.

Basic lemon dressing plus grated orange zest, honey, salt, and pepper.

OTHER DRESSINGS

1 par light soy sauce, 1 part rice vinegar, 2 parts olive oil, salt, and pepper.

1 part rice vinegar, 2 parts oil, a dash of sesame oil, freshly grated ginger, salt, and pepper.

1 part vinegar, 1 part oil, 2 parts light soy sauce, wasabi and crushed garlic.

Equal parts kimchi base, light soy sauce, white wine vinegar, oil, and grated fresh ginger.

STOCK

VEGETABLE STOCK
Fry 1 part sliced onion (yellow, red, or leek) and 2 parts chopped vegetables, such as celery root, carrots, or fennel, in a skillet with oil without browning. Cover with water, add herbs, including bay leaves and thyme, and a few white peppercorns. Simmer for 1 hour. Strain. Use immediately, refrigerate, or freeze.

EAT YOUR GREENS!
22 Ways to Cook a Carrot and 788 Other Delicious Recipes to Save the Planet

Text by Anette Dieng and Ingela Persson
Images by Erik Olsson
Edited by Robert Klanten and Lincoln Dexter

Translation from Swedish to English by Hilmir Thorisson

Design and illustrations by Katy Kimbell
Layout by gestalten
Typefaces: Rockwell, Super Grotesk

Printed by Printer Trento s.r.l., Trento
Made in Europe

Published by gestalten, Berlin 2020
ISBN 978-3-89955-999-6

5th printing, 2025

© 2017 Anette Dieng and Ingela Persson
Original title Skörd
First published by Natur & Kultur, Sweden
© for the English edition: gestalten, an imprint of
Die Gestalten Verlag GmbH & Co. KG, Berlin 2020

Copy-Editing by Julie Brooke, Sylvia Goulding, Chris Peterson, and Lesley Robb
Project management and typesetting by bookwise medienproduktion GmbH

All rights reserved. No part of this publication may be reproduced or transmitted in any form or by any means, electronic or mechanical, including photocopy or any storage and retrieval system, without permission in writing from the publisher.
No part of this book may be used or reproduced in any manner for the purpose of training artificial intelligence technologies or systems. This work is reserved from text and data mining (Article 4(3) Directive (EU) 2019/790).

Respect copyrights, encourage creativity!

For more information and to order books, please visit www.gestalten.com

Die Gestalten Verlag GmbH & Co. KG
Mariannenstrasse 9–10
10999 Berlin, Germany
hello@gestalten.com

Bibliographic information published by the Deutsche Nationalbibliothek. The Deutsche Nationalbibliothek lists this publication in the Deutsche Nationalbibliografie; detailed bibliographic data are available online at www.dnb.de.

This book was printed on paper certified according to the standards of the FSC®.